Don't Give Up on That Dog!

Raising a German Shepherd Dog:
The Many Lessons Learned

Kathy & Steve,
When one dog
wasn't enough,
we got a
real handful!
Hope you
enjoy!
Denine

Denine Phillips

Stoneledge
Press

Library of Congress Cataloging-in-Publication Data
Phillips, Denine.

Summary: A unique first-person account of day-to-day life with a
German shepherd, a story that will inspire new and future dog owners to
build the right foundation with their canine companion and, ultimately,
form an unbreakable bond. / Denine Phillips.
p. cm.

Includes bibliographical, web and photo credit references
1. German shepherd–New Jersey. 2. Dog–training. 3. Dog–behavior.
4. Human–animal relationships. 5. Raising a puppy.
I. Phillips, Denine. II. Title.

ISBN 978-0-615-55922-3

Design by Shannon Bodie, Lightbourne, Inc.

Printed in the United States

First Edition
Stoneledge Press, LLC

Praise For
DON'T GIVE UP ON THAT DOG!

"This book's value lies in the meticulous chronicling of all the different experiences a new dog owner can go through in a straightforward, clear way. And since the author is not pretending to be a professional dog trainer, the reader is able to place themselves in her shoes. The story is honest and reflects the wisdom of not giving up on a dog when one encounters difficulties."

—Brother Christopher Savage, *Author and Head Dog Trainer, The Monks of New Skete*

"People will relate to this book, a story of the average dog owner searching for ways to direct, harness and control a dog's energy—in a positive way. I would recommend this book for just the tips and advice alone. However, the events that unfold will make readers smile, as they see the many parallels. Though the book's title is, DON'T GIVE UP ON THAT DOG!, it could easily be subtitled, *You are not alone.*"

—Martin Deeley, *Executive Director, International Association of Canine Professionals*

"I've perused much of DON'T GIVE UP ON THAT DOG! and was completely engaged in what I read. It is immediately clear that the author's heart is in both the book and the dog."

—Wilma Melville, *Founder, National Disaster Search Dog Foundation & CNN Hero*

"This is a delightful book, with some extremely valuable lessons. It should be required reading for any first-time GSD owner. I wish I'd read it before I got my first shepherd."

—Amy Bures Danna, *Attorney, Animal Law Lecturer and Austin German Shepherd Rescue Volunteer*

"Whether you have a dog, cat or turtle, this is a beautiful story that captures the love between an animal and his owner, which helped me gain perspective on that bond, from an owner's point of view. I can't wait to read Part II of Cooper's journey!"

—Steve Hong, *World Competitor, Dog Trainer & Working-line German Shepherd Breeder*

"Love it! I hope that people will realize what it takes to raise a dog to its full potential. The rewards are limitless.

—Cheryl Smagala, *Dog Trainer*

"This book is a must-read for anyone who is thinking about getting a German shepherd, or any other breed of protective dog. Along with heart-warming stories—told with love and lots of humor, there are many helpful and easy to read 'Lessons Learned.' This book is engaging, educational and brought tears of joy as I cheered for Cooper's successes."

—Heidi Dabek

"Once I started reading, I was hooked. I really enjoyed the combination of storytelling and guide. It is a very cute story, and the dog raising and training tips make it a useful reference. The pictures are adorable, too. It's impossible not to fall in love with Cooper while reading about his shenanigans."

—Emily Waugh

"My wife and I found this book to be an excellent reference about raising a shepherd. Having brought ten shepherds into our home over the past three-plus decades, each was raised following the recommendations of the Monks of New Skete. What this book does is give readers day-to-day insights into ways to bring out the best in this noble breed."

—Michel Gélinas

"Cooper is one lucky dog. I love that he is living such a full life. It has also inspired me to do more with my shepherd."

—Debbie Crincoli

"Having had shepherds for 40 years, we just love this breed. Adorable Cooper… I love the pictures and the way his story is told."

—Linda Grefe

"I started reading after work today and couldn't stop. It is amazing how much we have in common being owners of German shepherds. They really are the best dogs!"

—Danielle Wells

*This book is dedicated to my loving family
who encouraged me to open up my heart
to another dog—a big dog.*

ABOUT THE BOOK

DON'T GIVE UP ON THAT DOG! is a true story that chronicles the many challenges faced while blending Cooper, a shy German Shepherd Dog, into a new family dynamic. Told with honesty and humor, this photo-filled journal of life with man *and* woman's best friend will inspire new and future dog owners to build the right foundation with their canine companion and, ultimately, form an unbreakable bond.

Under relentless pressure from her family to get another dog, the author *gets* far more than she bargained for—a fearful puppy that is terrified to explore the world. In the ensuing 16 months, she embarks on a mission to do whatever it takes to make Cooper a confident, trustworthy pack member.

Valuable lessons are learned along the way, some gleaned from expert dog trainers and behaviorists, as well as from first-hand experience. A vast array of book and article resources also provide a handy reference to those that wish to better understand the human-canine relationship.

The take-away message is that all dogs, particular guarding breeds, such as the Doberman pinscher, German shepherd, and Rottweiler, require skillful handling, with consistent rules and boundaries. The financial and emotional commitment can be enormous. However, staying the course—during the formative months—will reap rewards that far outweigh any sacrifices.

CONTENTS

INTRODUCTION 1

THE INSPIRATION 5
    Lessons Learned 10

MONTH 1: A NEW FAMILY DYNAMIC 13
    Lessons Learned 22

MONTH 2: SOCIALIZATION IN FULL SWING . . . 25
    Lessons Learned 31

MONTH 3: CLOSE ENCOUNTERS 33
    Lessons Learned 42

MONTH 4: THE EAR SAGA CONTINUES 45
    Lessons Learned 49

MONTH 5: BAD DOG! 51
    Lessons Learned 63

MONTH 6: DON'T GIVE UP ON THAT DOG! 67
    Lessons Learned 82

MONTH 7: A NEAR TRAGEDY 85
    Lessons Learned 92

MONTH 8: THE EARS? GIVE IT UP! 95
    Lessons Learned 99

MONTH 9: NO WATER DOG **101**
    Lessons Learned 107

MONTH 10: COOPER TURNS ONE **109**
    Lessons Learned 111

MONTH 11: THE ULTIMATE TEST **113**
    Lessons Learned 121

MONTH 12: DOG PARK REVISITED **123**
    Lessons Learned 129

MONTH 13: CANINE GOOD CITIZEN—
WHY NOT? **133**
    Lessons Learned 158

MONTH 14: POSITIVE DEVELOPMENTS **161**
    Lessons Learned 190

MONTH 15: GOOD DOG! **193**
    Lessons Learned 216

CONCLUSION **219**

AFTERWORD **221**

    Words of Wisdom 225
    Acknowledgements 227
    Book & Article Resources 229
    Web Resources 230
    About the Author 233

INTRODUCTION

In the summer of 2009, pressure was mounting. Not from the rising thermometer but from my family. They desperately wanted another dog. Our beloved golden retriever, Sidney, had died in February. Sidney's daughter had died three months prior. Having suffered through back-to-back losses of our furry friends, I declared, "No more dogs!" Our daughter, Amy, had just returned home after four years away at college. Bring another dog into the mix? Out of the question! I really put my foot down, which is surprising coming from a life-long animal lover.

Indeed, my job as a freelance technical writer masks my first love—animals. As a child, I accumulated a menagerie of critters—gerbils, mice, horny toads, chameleons, you name it. I even earned a degree in Biology from Rutgers University, hoping I could put that focus and energy to good use, perhaps as a veterinarian. Fast forward 35 years and my husband, John, and I are looking toward retirement. How old would we be when we say good-bye to this dog—in our 60s? We want to travel and enjoy our golden years. Being free of all responsibility, we could enjoy the great outdoors by way of a shiny new Airstream travel trailer.

Not so fast! Those plans did not align with John and Amy's hopes for the future. Instead, I heard over and over, "We need a dog, a big dog!" They had to make the "big dog" distinction, since we have a little dog, Ozzie. Ozzie is a Shih Tzu that fulfilled my need for a lap dog, a decade earlier. There is only one problem: Ozzie is not a *real* dog. One family friend described him as a masculine cat. Amy concurred, saying, "We need a big dog that I can teach tricks, go running with, and that would enjoy riding in the car." These are all things that Ozzie doesn't do. He has no interest in doing tricks, could not possibly handle a three-mile run and does not do stairs. Just getting into the car, much less riding in it, makes his little body shake uncontrollably. Don't get me wrong, Ozzie is very sweet and cuddly. He does not, however, fill the "big dog" void in our home.

While John and Amy pined for a big dog, there was a full-blown puppy population explosion in our immediate circle. One of Amy's friends brought home a pit bull puppy, something that did not sit well with his mother. But the puppy, Maddie, was cute, smart and playful; Amy was smitten. Shortly thereafter another friend brought home a boxer puppy; a ball of energy if I've ever seen one.

Prior to my meeting these pups, Amy's good friend acquired a Doberman pinscher puppy, Kona. Amy puppy-sat for Kona at our house, supervising her outdoor explorations and laughing as she did figure eights through my garden. Despite Kona laying waste to the perennial plants, I began

thinking maybe we could do this again. Clearly, my "No dog!" stance was weakening, despite a dog's obvious destructive tendencies.

Amy is used to having a dog underfoot. We brought home our third golden retriever puppy when she was just seven years old; there was a lull after our first set of goldens died. We waited, as Amy needed to be old enough to handle a rambunctious puppy. She named her Belle, from Disney's fairy tale *Beauty and the Beast*. Over the ensuing 18-plus years, we have had four more retrievers, even breeding for a number of years. Another big dog in the house? Been there, done that.

Trying to keep an open mind, I began to take baby steps, asking Amy, "How about raising a dog for the Seeing Eye?" She had expressed interest during her high school years, so she set out to learn more. If she did volunteer, she wanted to raise a German shepherd puppy—something different than the ubiquitous Labrador or golden retriever. That would be perfect! We would have a dog, but only temporarily. When push came to shove, however, Amy could not imagine letting go of a dog, especially one that she had spent months training. That exercise did focus her attention on the breed of dog she would like—a German shepherd, a faithful companion that would sleep beside her bed.

While I never committed to anything, I began secretly gathering information on German shepherds. Words commonly used to describe the breed—intelligent, loyal, protective—all sounded great. With a shepherd, we would have the added benefit of a guardian, a sentry that would alert us to people at the door or ward off burglars lurking in the bushes, neither of which were pressing concerns. There are doorbells and alarm systems for that. Nonetheless, I forged ahead. The only thing I was absolutely sure of was that I needed to be 100-percent on board with choosing a dog. Surely, I'll be the one assuming dog-care duties, despite promises to the contrary. Feeding, walking, training, vet visits and innumerable other activities would be mine. Without my buy-in, things might not go so well.

As summer turned to fall, and we settled into our respective routines, I said to John, "How about surprising Amy with a puppy?" Being an only child, I spoil her far too much—even after 22 years. Since she had taken a serious interest in running, a big dog could accompany her on long outings. Knowing that she is not alone would bring me a degree of comfort, and possibly justify the decision to get another big dog. Alas, I had cracked.

THE INSPIRATION

"Beginning is easy—continuing hard."

—Japanese proverb

-2009-
OCTOBER 16

Barb and I were on a 2-mile power walk when we crossed paths with a gentleman and his two dogs. One dog was clearly a shepherd. I was not sure of the other dog's breed. Though we have exchanged pleasantries on many occasions, this time I couldn't let him pass. I had to meet these dogs, particularly the one with beautiful coloring and plush coat. As we slowed down, I asked, "Are they friendly?" He said, "Yes." As I extended my hand, the handsome long-coat sprang up, planting his wet nose directly in my face. It was a friendly gesture—no harm done—but the owner gave a quick correction with the leash.

For fear of being rude, I introduced myself and Barb. The gentleman's name was Michel. With formalities out of the way, I asked him about the dogs' breed, knowing full well that the short-coat dog was a shepherd. When pointing to the long-coat, he said, "He's a shepherd, too." His name was Pancho, after Pancho Villa, the Mexican revolutionary leader. I had no idea that the breed produced long coats. The silkiness of the fur reminded me of our many goldens, only Pancho was black and tan. I asked, "Where did you get him?" Given Michel's French accent, I feared he had gotten the dog from overseas. To my surprise, he said, "Valley Crest Kennel." The facility was located only 20 minutes away, so I might be in luck. I was anxious to get back to my office. With a quick Google search, there they were. I shot off an e-mail message to the kennel owner....

To: Valley Crest Kennel
From: D. Phillips

I had the pleasure of meeting one of your gorgeous shepherds, Pancho. He's owned by a neighbor of ours. Do you still breed the same line? We are not in a hurry for a puppy. Instead, I prefer to wait for the right match. We lost our golden retriever earlier in the year, and this is my first time inquiring about another "family member." Thanks and look forward to hearing from you.

OCTOBER 17

Opening my e-mail this morning, I was so hoping that the kennel would respond to my inquiry. They did! Amazingly, they have one puppy left, an 8-week-old, long-coat male— just what I wanted. Apparently, the puppy had been sold to a gentleman who recently lost his job. We may have found our puppy far faster than I had imagined. Even if he's the runt of the litter, that's fine. We have no basis for comparison. We're set to visit the kennel tomorrow afternoon.

OCTOBER 18

John and I pulled into the kennel parking lot right on time, 1:00 p.m. Having seen many dog breeding operations in the past, this facility was, without a doubt, the nicest. Our pet searches have taken us to places that left much to be desired. In contrast, the main house was a stately stone colonial, with manicured grounds, ample customer parking and an impressive expanse of chain-link enclosures that looked brand new.

We were greeted at the door by the kennel owner, Jill. There were also three other people in attendance, including the puppy owner, Lynn. Not to be overlooked was a very calm, older female shepherd, perhaps their ambassador for the breed. But my focus was really on the rather large group that had gathered in the room, which I'll admit was intimidating. Jill began by explaining her breeding philosophy, practices, and the expectations for owners of her dogs, including the mandatory purchase of vitamins, through her. John and I listened politely. Lynn then went to get the puppy. Since she lives in Pennsylvania, it was easier for her to bring the pup to New Jersey. Unfortunately, that did not afford us the opportunity to meet the puppy's parents. Buying a puppy without getting a sense of the sire and dam's temperament was against my better judgment. I asked about hip certification, which is available through the Orthopedic Foundation for Animals (OFA), but we were told that X-rays can be of any dog. We didn't press this issue either; we were clearly caught up in the moment.

As Lynn emerged from the basement with the lone puppy, he was just what I imagined—a ball of fluffy black and tan fur with huge paws. Setting off an abundance of cuteness was a multi-color bow made of yarn. It was love at first sight. Lynn dropped the little guy in my arms. He fidgeted until I placed him on the ground, for fear of dropping him; he made a hasty retreat. Lynn scooped him up and placed him back in my arms. Looking into those sad but beautiful eyes, your mind no longer functions properly. We should have asked questions about the puppy's parents. What were their temperaments like? Were there any known hereditary problems? At the very least, John and I should have gone outside to talk things over. Instead, we spent our time trying to connect with the shy puppy. As he ran away from us, there was no doubt about his bond with Lynn, which was to be expected. Needless to say, we were soon owners of a German shepherd. Since we are no beginners at raising puppies, what could possibly go wrong?

When we got home, the puppy was naturally nervous. We did our best to ease his separation anxiety, placing him in his crate with a blanket on top for a quiet, den-like setting. As John and I relaxed in the living room, he crept ever so slowly out of the kitchen, making his way toward me. I picked him up, trying in vain to comfort him. Rather than resting in my arms, he preferred to lie on the floor with his head hidden under the ottoman.

As he slept at my feet, Amy arrived home. She had no idea what she was about to see. Even before reaching the living room archway, she looked down and gasped, "Oh, my gosh!" and sprinted toward the startled puppy. Amy plopped to the floor, whisking him up into her arms. I only wish I had a picture of the astonished look on her face, as she exclaimed, "A German shepherd puppy?" I nodded, yes. She cried. I cried.

LESSONS LEARNED

✔ Inquire with veterinarians, dog trainers and dog training clubs about local breeders. These professionals have a wealth of knowledge that can be invaluable.

✔ Visit several breeders. I suspect that many people spend more time researching new appliances than choosing a breeder; keep your options open by visiting two or more kennels.

✔ As Martin Deeley, internationally renowned dog trainer says, "Selecting a puppy is a lifetime commitment for the pup, and dog ownership is not a responsibility to be taken lightly." To see his tips on picking a puppy go to *www. martindeeley.com* (click the *Articles* link).

Take emotion out of the equation by taking a day or two to sleep on the decision to bring a puppy home. You have to be certain it's the right move for your family. As Bruce Fogle, DMV, says, "Control your impulse to buy the first puppy that catches your eye; it may very well be the best, but you can only be sure after seeing others."

✔ While pet stores are another option, as are large-scale breeding operations, a.k.a. puppy mills, the principal of *caveat emptor* applies—let the buyer beware.

✔ Another option is to rescue a dog from an experienced rescue group or established animal shelter, though having experience with protective breeds, such as shepherds, is highly recommended.

✔ Ask if a puppy can be returned within the first year due to crippling dysplasia or unsound temperament. Typically, breeders allow 48 hours for a veterinary exam, and subsequent return of a sick puppy, but this added clause is desirable. And just like cars, there is a Lemon Law for puppies. For information on Puppy Lemon Laws visit *www.njcapsa.org.*

✔ Ask about any known hereditary problems in the puppy's bloodlines, such as:

▪ Poor temperament. Meet the puppy's parents (sire and dam). Only then can you gauge whether or not the line is of sound temperament. The environment the puppies were raised in can also be determined. Is it clean? Was there early socialization with people and other animals? One local breeder socializes her puppies before their eyes even open, playing audio recordings of thunder, fireworks, barking dogs, babies crying, anything  that could later frighten a dog. (More on noise desensitization will follow.)

▪ Hip Dysplasia. According to research at the University of Pennsylvania, hip dysplasia is present in all breeds of dog, so ask if the sire and dam have been certified by the Orthopedic Foundation for Animals (OFA). To view statistics of the prevalence of hip dysplasia by breed, visit *http://offa.org/stats_hip.html*. You can learn about elbow dysplasia as well.

▪ Cancer. Hemangiosarcoma, for instance, is a disease that occurs most commonly in large-breed dogs. The tumors are highly malignant and can be found anywhere in the dog's body, and is usually seen in dogs eight years of age and older.

- Megaesophagus. This disease makes it difficult for a puppy to pass food from the esophagus to the stomach, causing regurgitation back into the throat. This condition, which can be present in certain bloodlines, can also develop later in a dog's life.
- Rage Syndrome. This is an extremely rare condition, but is nonetheless worth asking about. Rage Syndrome is described as aggression that comes out of nowhere. It is, in fact, an epileptic seizure in the emotional lobe of a dog's brain.

✔ Ask about other maladies, including seizure disorders, allergies, hypothyroidism, bloat, pancreatic and kidney problems, mitral valve murmurs, and other heart-related disorders.Though most reputable breeders will honestly answer questions about health and behavioral issues, they may also be dismissive, perhaps even offended. The truth is that there is no guarantee that any puppy will develop into a healthy adult dog. All you can do is prepare yourself by knowing as much about the bloodlines as possible. Consider it an exercise in due diligence.

MONTH 1:
A NEW FAMILY DYNAMIC

"When you look at your life, the greatest happinesses are family happinesses."

—Joyce Brothers

OCTOBER 19

The first order of business: a trip to Dr. Reynolds' office, our long-time, trusted veterinarian. If an exam should reveal any health problems or congenital defects, we could return the puppy to the breeder. That window is only open for two days, so we needed to act right away. Having caved to John and Amy's demand for a puppy, I thought I would test their

willingness to pitch in by asking them to take the dog to the vet. Having always assumed that role, I was pleasantly surprised when they agreed. Upon their return, our new buddy was just fine. All systems go. The only thing that concerned me was Dr. Reynolds' opinion about his ears. They are so large that he doesn't believe there is enough cartilage to support them in

adulthood. And before leaving, he inquired about our choosing a shepherd, after 30-plus years of goldens. Amy explained that we wanted a change. Dr. Reynolds, with his wonderful wry sense of humor, said, "I never got a German shepherd because I didn't want a dog that was smarter than me."

Now we needed to give the puppy a name. We threw around the customary choices—Bear, Duke, Buster, Prince, but Amy came up with a name she really liked—Cooper. She drove home from work behind a BMW MINI Cooper automobile. Wanting her to take ownership, so to speak, John and I gave a thumbs-up. *Cooper* it is.

Cooper whimpered on and off all night, as expected. The key was to not cuddle him in response. I held out, until whining turned into continuous barking. That's when I took him outside

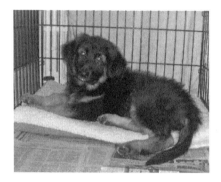

to do his business. After being placed back in his crate, he settled down. I would have loved to keep him in a crate near the bed, but dogs or cats in the bedroom never allow for a good night's sleep— at least for me.

OCTOBER 20

Cooper has had a few days to adjust to his new home, so Amy and I took him on his first errand—buy more puppy food, a collar and toys. The breeder was feeding him large breed puppy food. For big dogs, my understanding is that a formula for large dogs allows them to grow more slowly, which is best for healthy development. Off we went to the pet store.

As we strolled through the aisles with Cooper, Amy stopped to admire the cutest little yellow Labrador puppy. We began talking to the woman and her teenage daughter. Their puppy was from the Seeing Eye in Morristown. They are training the pup for the next 16 months, which means lots of socialization. Despite the puppy's diminutive size, she had Cooper pinned on his back within seconds.

As the puppies played, the woman told us how she would never train another shepherd puppy for the Seeing Eye. Apparently, the dog bonded to her daughter; he would not listen to anyone but her. I saw that human-canine connection as a positive trait in a service dog, but she was not to be dissuaded. We could have done without that story, since Cooper is ours. We can't give him back.

OCTOBER 22

A smart puppy indeed, Cooper is already getting the hang of doing his business outside. I carry him to *his* spot and use a simple command, "Hurry up." When he complies, he gets a treat; good behavior is always rewarded. Very soon, when he is a little bigger, he'll be able to handle the patio steps on his own.

Houseplants were something I had completely forgotten about. I had an African violet and dieffenbachia within easy reach, both of which are poisonous to dogs. Though Cooper had shown no interest in chewing on anything other than his toys, I took all of the houseplants to the basement. He can't navigate those steps either.

OCTOBER 24

Brushing Cooper has been a near-daily ritual. His long coat needs serious tending to, but he wants no part of this foreign object—the brush. He bites at the brush and frantically tries to escape my clutches. I lay him on his side and gently run the brush over his back and down his tail. By the time it reaches the end of his back, it's an all-out battle. There's only one way to handle this situation, repeat the process over and over. He'll learn that nothing bad will happen. In fact, he'll one day come to enjoy the attention. Our goldens loved being brushed, and Skipper, our first golden, loved nothing more than to be vacuumed.

OCTOBER 26

John brought home a book, *The Art of Raising a Puppy*, written by the Monks of New Skete, in New York state. It was a gift from his customers, Max and Jean, who have owned many shepherds, most recently Heidi, a friendly dog that sits watch over their 140-acre dairy farm. They considered this book the best ever written on the topic of raising a well-mannered dog. I was intrigued because the Monks specialize in German shepherd training and breeding.

Heidi was John's constant companion while he painted Max and Jean's home. Lunchtime was especially fun for Heidi, as she eagerly awaited scraps of food tossed her way. One day, while John was sitting on his van bumper, enjoying his sandwich, a young heifer approached, a friendly cow that was allowed to roam free. With the cow and shepherd competing for handouts, John was in a pickle. The problem was soon solved when the 1,000-pound cow chased Heidi clear across the front yard. It all happened so fast; John sprinted around the side of his van to see if Heidi was okay. All was well, and the heifer was soon back at John's side; Heidi kept her distance.

OCTOBER 29

One of our concerns was how Cooper would treat Ozzie, our 10-year-old Shih Tzu. Being three times his size, I had expected Cooper to trample him. That has not been the case. Cooper defers to Ozzie, perhaps as the elder pack member. Ozzie is clearly the more dominant dog. Little Ozzie growls at Cooper, even as he's stealing Cooper's food. I correct Ozzie with a firm "No!" and he backs off—returning to his own bowl. Cooper appears to have no food or dog aggression; he goes with the flow.

NOVEMBER 1

Having a cat in the house has presented real challenges. I should have learned my lesson as a child and be wary of bringing a vocal Siamese cat into the house, but Amy adores Meeko. A curious puppy, Cooper has turned Meeko's world upside down. Since Ozzie totally ignores Cooper, where is a puppy to turn? Meeko, however, is not embracing this new reality; he'll have none of it. I keep Meeko's nails cut very short, to minimize injury to Cooper's substantial nose. Yelling "No!" as he chases the cat through the house has been  ineffective. My hope is that Cooper and Meeko will soon become friends, though that may be overly optimistic.

NOVEMBER 5

From the day we brought Cooper home, his oversized crate (which sits in our high-traffic kitchen), has been his favorite resting place. We make it a happy place, tossing treats in and then closing the door whenever we need to leave the house. Even without enticement, he goes in to rest or chew on toys. But as I quickly learned, the crate had an unknown danger, the curved metal latch that secures the cage when folded. Cooper got his lower jaw caught on the latch. Letting out an ear-piercing cry, he struggled to free himself. If I had not been sitting in the kitchen, I fear what could have happened, as he thrashed in his cage, a broken jaw at the very least. I was able to lift his body and angle his jaw free. The adrenalin was still rushing through me as I angrily took pliers to the latch, permanently removing the hazard.

NOVEMBER 10

Amy and I took Cooper to his first Puppy Kindergarten class. Amy took the reins, so to speak. I sat on the sidelines. Cooper, however, was not pleased. He strained and barked in

a relentless effort to get to me. Amy handled him well, but I won't be going to the remaining classes. Cooper had to stay focused. With another dog in the class named Cooper, that was no easy feat.

Before class ended, we were instructed to introduce our puppy to a minimum of 100 people over the course of the class, and before "graduating." No problem. We have Cooper out and about often. It's astonishing how people are attracted to him, peppering us with questions. Among the top queries: "Is he a mixed breed?" and "Did you rescue him?" While the first question was easy to answer, since people are not usually aware that shepherd genetics include long coats. "Did you rescue him?" sounded like a loaded question. I said, "No. We got him from a breeder." That seemed to disappoint those that feel there are too many dogs in need of homes to buy one. I really can't argue that point.

NOVEMBER 11

With Puppy Kindergarten requirements in the back of my mind, Cooper and I headed to town. On this first formal excursion, I logged 27 people who visited with Cooper, from only two activities—a visit to the pet store and a spin up and down Main Street. Later, while romping in the yard, we also practiced Target, a game Amy played with Cooper in class. The puppy sees you place a treat some distance away. You then give the "Target" command, and the puppy rushes to that spot. As he snatches up the treat, I say, "Cooper, come!" The key is to get him to come back by calling his name. When he complies, and is sitting straight in front of me, I give him another treat. Not only is he learning his name, he is seeking something when given a command. Before long, Cooper should be coming to me whenever called, so treats will always be at hand.

At this stage, Amy and I are having difficulty holding Cooper on our lap for three minutes, an exercise that is supposed to show Cooper who's the boss—the alpha dog. The alpha dog is everyone in the house but him. When placed on his back, he struggles with all his might. While I feel bad

for him, as he fusses and whines, Amy assures me that we are not hurting him. It's important that we practice this exercise on a daily basis, until Cooper no longer resists.

Another lesson we learned is Tie-down, which we used this evening during dinner. Cooper is okay with this, as we secure his leash to an immovable object—a 200-pound cast iron radiator. Eventually we will be able to simply say, "Go lie down," without using the leash.

NOVEMBER 16

Cooper's favorite toys are large balls, like Amy's old soccer ball and volleyball. He is not much bigger than the ball, but when Amy threw them into his pen, Cooper took off in hot pursuit. Maybe they look like very round sheep. As he plays, we have the added pleasure of seeing him trot. I liken it to a horse in dressage. This graceful gait is called the Flying Trot, a wonderful characteristic of the breed.

November 18

I decided to meet Amy at Puppy Kindergarten, during puppy playtime. Unfortunately, Cooper was focused on just one thing—getting to me. In the process, he crashed through the flimsy PVC barrier keeping the dogs separated from their owners. It was painful to watch. He was so miserable, as was Molly, his littermate. Unlike Cooper, Molly did engage in some play, but she had her eye on the exit as well. That was not money well spent. Cooper is clearly not interested in frolicking with other puppies.

LESSONS LEARNED

✔ Read books about the proper care and training of a puppy. Even if you have raised dogs in the past, there is always something new to learn from the experts, like the Monks of New Skete (*www.newskete.com*). Another great source of information is the AKC website (*www.akc.org*).

✔ Before bringing a puppy home, survey the house. Remove poisonous houseplants. Tie up electrical and blind cords and secure them out of sight. Put away any hazards sitting on counters or tables. For more information on keeping your puppy safe, visit *www. peteducation.com*.

> There are many different choices when it comes to puppy food. If you choose to change the brand of food, the process must be gradual, over a week or so.

✔ Examine other sources of danger, even the puppy's crate. Remove any metal or plastic pieces on the inside of the crate, which might snag the jaw of a teething puppy.

✔ Have plenty of dog toys lying around. It may save the furniture. For added measure, I rubbed Tabasco sauce on the rungs of our kitchen and dining room chairs. One sniff and he gets the message.

✔ Take the puppy for car rides. The sooner he learns to travel in the car the better, as this early experience in a moving vehicle can prevent car sickness down the road.

✔ Expose the puppy to all types of people, young and old, as well as other animals. For instance, once the puppy has all his inoculations, take him for a walk in town or through the park. People are instantly attracted to puppies, so this early socialization is easy. At the same time, you meet very interesting people, many who have their own stories of dog ownership.

✓ Basic obedience needs to begin right away, so check for Puppy Kindergarten classes in your area. I had no idea this type of class existed. But only one handler should go to class. As much as a family member might want to watch, the presence of an additional person can be a distraction. If you don't attend a formal class, practice sit, stay, down and come every day. Short sessions are all that's needed. With a treat in your hand, a puppy is a very fast learner.

✓ Brushing a puppy on a daily basis is not only the responsible thing to do, it will help him overcome any fear of grooming. Cooper wants no part of this process, but slow and steady is the name of this game.

✓ Use a simple phrase or word when housetraining a puppy. When Cooper goes out, I say, "Hurry up." Works beautifully. And when you're away from home, those same words help the dog to understand when it's time to get down to business.

✓ Crate training is so important. It makes housebreaking a puppy far easier, and saves you the headache of cleaning up after the dog lays waste to your home. And since the puppy views the crate as a den, he will naturally gravitate to the security and quiet of his own space. A good source for information on crate training is the Humane Society website (*www.humanesociety.org*).

Month 2: Socialization In Full Swing

> "A puppy is extremely sensitive to socializing experiences between three and twelve weeks of age, when their effects are permanent for better or worse."
>
> —*The Monks of New Skete*

November 20

John needed some supplies from Home Depot, so Cooper and I went along for the ride. John entered the store; we stood outside the sliding exit doors. All of the commotion was good for Cooper. Since he's in that cute puppy stage, people gathered around. At one point five people stood in front of us. They asked, "What kind of dog is he?" "Is he a mix?" And there was the very common, "Look at those big paws!" He'll be a big dog!" One couple actually identified Cooper's breed, long-coat German shepherd. Most people I've met over the past few weeks have never seen a long-coat shepherd. But while I answered people's questions, I encouraged Cooper to "Say hello," as he was doing his best to hide behind me. Not wanting to push him too much, he sat quietly until John emerged. I can see that Cooper is going to need many more outings like this one.

NOVEMBER 25

John wanted to see his brother Rich's new Camaro, so we headed to Readington. My hope was that Cooper could meet their boys, Nick, Kyle and Brian; only 11-year-old Brian was home, but that was good. He greeted Cooper, though their dog Jack, an older beagle, was not pleased. As John and Rich drove off, I turned my attention to the neighbor's yard, where a golden retriever was playing. Donna, Rich's wife, asked her neighbors if we could come over and meet Brandy. She said, "Sure!" Brandy was a delightful dog. At 10 years old, she was still very playful. Though there was a substantial size difference, Cooper took an immediate liking to her. And while she repeatedly took Cooper down, with some force, he bounced right back. The only embarrassing moment was when Cooper left a sizable deposit in their backyard. It was a great trip for Cooper. The more enjoyable dog and human interactions he experiences the better.

NOVEMBER 26

Thanksgiving Day! Amy ran in the Annual Turkey Trot, a 5K race. Her Uncle Stuart, who is also a runner, was there as well. I encouraged John to take Cooper, so they could cheer

Amy and Stu on. That also gave me breathing room in the kitchen.

After they returned home, and before hearing how the race went, John said, "Cooper got loose in town." Apparently, he had lost his grip on the leash. All three of them laughed as they told how Cooper was running wild through the crowd of runners and spectators. I didn't see much humor in this, but when they said there were no moving cars in sight, I calmed down. I thought John had nearly killed Cooper. Instead, they were in hysterics telling how they all were yelling, "Catch that dog!" People sprang into action, but no one could catch him. Cooper was headed for his own car, and that is where they finally caught him.

After that episode, John held on tight to Cooper's leash as they made their way back into town to watch the race. Cooper was what John and Stu called a "chick magnet." Everyone wanted to stop and say hello. Disaster averted, it was another day out for Cooper.

NOVEMBER 30

We had a wicked thunderstorm, which gave me an opportunity to observe how Cooper would react to rattling windows and flashing lights. Whenever Sidney (our previous dog) would hear a thunder clap, she tried desperately to squeeze her 80-pound body behind the couch. Ozzie is also terrified of thunder. His goal: get to the highest peak—which is the top of the stairs. That's odd because Ozzie, otherwise, does not do stairs. And there's one problem, he cannot get back down. It was years before we knew what was going on. We would look all over for him, only to find him cowering at the top of the landing.

For Cooper, the storm didn't have any affect. What a relief. Cooper behaved just like Nicki, Sidney's daughter; she couldn't have cared less. Why one dog goes into a frenzy, while another is indifferent, I am at a loss to explain.

DECEMBER 4

Cooper is doing great… growing like a weed. And this weekend, he gets his picture taken for the Valley Crest Kennel 2010 Calendar. People can vote on-line for their favorite dog, so we will hope Cooper makes the grade. If not, a photo of all the dogs is still on the calendar, so everyone wins.

DECEMBER 6

I arrived at the kennel at 12:00 p.m. for Cooper's photo shoot. Cooper's littermate, Molly, and her owners, Bob and Susan, were already there. Cooper and Molly instantly recognized one another. In the chaos of puppies bouncing about and intertwined leashes, we promised to get the dogs together at a later date. Cooper was summoned in for his picture.

It was a struggle from the get-go; Cooper had no interest in sitting in front of the decorative backdrop. The photographer was patient, taking at least two dozen pictures. I'm hoping for one good one. We were then directed to the next room to purchase packages of photos. I opted for just the calendar; proceeds of which will go to a local animal shelter.

DECEMBER 14

Cooper graduated from Puppy Kindergarten tonight, complete with Certificate of Achievement. Molly had already finished this class, but had stopped by for playtime. Again, Cooper was not having any of it—the playtime, that is. Amy took Cooper through the entire 6-week program, and Cooper performed extremely well, with the instructor often using them to demonstrate exercises. It has helped them bond. I hope she will take him on to higher-level obedience training.

DECEMBER 16

I took Cooper to be evaluated at doggy daycare. I wasn't familiar with these facilities, since the goldens had been more gregarious and outgoing. In comparison, Cooper is very shy. Daycare might be the best move. Exposing Cooper to different people, places and dogs might help him emerge from his shell. We met Linda, the owner, who led us into the main indoor play area. Everything was clean and orderly, but that unmistakable dog odor was strong. She and her assistant tried to interact with Cooper, but he was timid. They gave him time, letting him investigate the room before introducing a small, friendly dog. Cooper greeted the dog, no problem. The next dog was led in, a slightly larger dog. Again, no problem, but no real interaction either. They finally called for Sophie to come in from the outdoor  run. A beautiful red standard poodle, Sophie, came bounding into the room. It was not long before Cooper fell in love. They really hit it off. Having passed the test, by virtue of his submissiveness, we were given an application and medical forms to fill out. Once I get the paperwork in order, along with proof of vaccinations and negative stool sample, Cooper will be frolicking with friends—at least one day a week.

DECEMBER 18

Cooper had his first-ever dog park experience. A friend had mentioned a large open space, designated just for dogs. I wanted to see how Cooper would handle himself. He has been exposed to other dogs in training. What could go wrong? As I approached the chain-link area, with double-gated entry, I noticed just one other dog—a very large Doberman pinscher. I asked the woman, who was wearing a jacket with New Jersey State Trooper insignia, if her dog was friendly. Her response, "Oh, yes." As we entered, the Doberman raced over to greet Cooper, who tolerated being poked in his private parts—just a way dogs greet one another. They did seem to get along just fine, but what I thought was play was really Cooper trying to get away. He ran as fast as he could, but the enormous Doberman toppled him. This went on for about five minutes. After one take-down, Cooper hit the ground hard, right on his back. He yelped. That was it. I quickly gathered him up and left. Cooper needs another 50 pounds before he can tussle with *that* big dog.

DECEMBER 19

Perhaps it was too soon, but I took Cooper for a walk down to the river. Without hesitation, he trotted alongside me. The first part of our journey, downhill, was a breeze. On the return trip, uphill, he was lagging behind. And as he jumped at my side, as if asking to get picked up, I felt bad. He was really too heavy to haul back home, so he had to tough it out. I'll wait a few more weeks before trying that again.

LESSONS LEARNED

✔ A shy German shepherd may require years of socialization. Cooper frequently visits big box stores, pet shops, parks, homes of family and friends. For those living in New Jersey, the book *Happy Tails Across New Jersey, Things to See and Do with Your Dog in the Garden State*, by Diane Goodspeed, is a county-by-county guide with a wealth of information about fun places to take your dog.

✔ Always wrap the loop of the puppy's leash through your hand. As we learned, even a 6-foot, 190-pound man can lose his grip on a leash. *Note*: You'll notice professional dog handlers put the right thumb through the loop of the leash and (with the dog heeling on their left) control the dog with the leash gathered around their left wrist, to take up slack. For me, I just do what's comfortable, as long as Cooper isn't running circles around me, I'm happy.

✔ I'm not a fan of retractable leashes; they are fine for small dogs. For a large-breed dog, they do not provide enough control. Case in point: as Amy walked Buddy (one of our goldens), the dog pulled a retractable leash handle out of her hand. As it crashed to the concrete sidewalk, Buddy ran for the hills. After 10 agonizing days, John found the dog in a dry river bed— emaciated and covered in ticks, but alive.

If your dog has fears issues associated with certain noises, like thunder and fireworks, check out Canine Noise Phobia™ Series, which are clinically researched sound effects designed to desensitize a dog. For more information, go to *http:// throughadogsear.com*.

✔ Take a puppy to doggy daycare. Cooper is able

to safely interact with other people and dogs that have been screened for any signs of aggression. By taking him out of his comfort zone—our home—we hope he will grow into a confident dog.

✔ A no-cost alternative to doggy daycare is a dog park, but be very careful. At the very least, the facility should be separated by dog size—small, medium and large.

✔ Limit your walk with a puppy to short distances. Regrettably, I took Cooper on a journey he was not prepared to take.

Month 3:
Close Encounters

**"When we are afraid we ought not to occupy
ourselves with endeavoring to prove that there
is no danger, but in strengthening ourselves
to go on in spite of the dangers."**

—*Mark Rutherford*

December 21

Today was bitter cold, even by December standards. But weather does not bother Cooper. He was more than happy to accompany me on a mission to swap cars with Amy. She was working the evening shift at Borders Books, and needed all-wheel drive for the trip home, as the weather forecast had predicted six inches of snow that evening. Her small sedan would never make it. Cooper and I walked up and down the sidewalk waiting for Amy, as people admired the puppy with the big paws. When I could no longer feel *my* toes, we entered the store's vestibule to warm up.

There were people streaming in and out; Christmas was just four days away. Cooper sat by my side, watching intently as the crushing crowd passed by. He appeared nervous as we tried to make way for shoppers, alternating between yawning and clinching his jaws. I tightened my grip on the leash, Cooper surely sensed my discomfort.

Within just a few minutes, a women and her son, in his late 20s, entered the store. What happened next was bewildering. The man dropped to the floor, crossed his legs and began talking directly to Cooper. "What's your name? How old are you? You're going to be a big boy!" The one-sided conversation didn't stop. I quickly realized that he was a person with special needs. Not to be rude, I tried to help answer his questions, while not blocking people trying to navigate around him.

What a predicament! As I'm trying to balance this man's need to engage with Cooper, with my need to get out of there, a father with his two small children passed within inches of Cooper's substantial nose, and equally substantial teeth. That's when I heard a low growl—a clear signal that Cooper was uncomfortable in such tight quarters. I abruptly said, "We've got to get going now. Nice talking to you," and made a bee-line for the door.

At only four months of age, Cooper has shown a dangerous sign, a fear of small children, a trait that was very worrisome. When I told John and Amy about the encounter, they dismissed it as Cooper being in a strange setting, not a behavioral issue. I was unnerved by the event, replaying the scene in my head. Is this a harbinger of things to come?

DECEMBER 22

John and Amy took Cooper for his last set of puppy shots. Besides the standard shots, we included a vaccination for Lyme disease, which is prevalent in our area. We also chose to microchip Cooper, a procedure to insert a tiny chip between his shoulder blades, using a hypodermic needle. A recent story about Duke, a one-year-old shepherd, influenced my decision. Duke ran away and was never found. The family was heartbroken.

Since I couldn't go along, I asked John to question Dr. Reynolds about Cooper's relentless harassment of the cat. On any given day, Meeko responds by taking vicious swipes at Cooper, who isn't being aggressive, just curious. My question for Dr. Reynolds: "Is there a chill pill we could give the cat?" When John and Amy returned, they got great satisfaction out of Dr. Reynolds' response. He said, "Maybe *she* needs a chill pill," meaning me. I got my answer, and a good laugh.

DECEMBER 23

Cooper's breeder, Lynn, offered a complimentary grooming for Cooper. I took her up on the offer, dropping Cooper off in the morning. When I picked him up, I was astonished at the improvement—all loose fur was gone, his paws were trimmed, and the glossy finish to his coat was accentuated by a new winter-themed bandana wrapped around his neck. That kind gesture was deserving of both homemade cookies and a sizable tip.

DECEMBER 24

Getting ready for Christmas! Being out and about more than usual, Cooper was eager to join me on my many missions—Walmart, ShopRite… anywhere I was going, he wanted to be. I lifted him into the back seat, and off we went. He sat quietly, seemingly content to do absolutely nothing. From time to time, he tried to peer out the window, but just kicking back was more his style.

After our shopping trip, we headed down to my mother's apartment. Cooper was getting much better at navigating the stairs that lead to her front door. He was eager to enter, since cat food was readily available. I'm sure my mother hates that. If it's a full bowl, however, I do swoop in before Cooper can get to it.

Cooper was still a bit hesitant when it comes to seeing Mom. Being elderly, she has a variety of assistive devices, like canes that frequently crash to the floor and a squeaky walker, things Cooper tiptoes around. To ease him into every visit, I had Mom give him biscuits. He has to sit nicely, and is then rewarded. It won't take long for Cooper to be desensitized to all the new sights and sounds.

- 2010-
JANUARY 3

For the first time, I realized that Cooper doesn't destroy anything. In the past, our golden puppies would chew shoes, socks, curtains, carpet, couch cushions, anything and everything. Cooper is still teething, but appears to be content with his toys, not our possessions. We have even started leaving him loose in the house at night. This would have been impossible with our other dogs.

JANUARY 4

While our first trip to the dog park didn't go so well, my fear was that Cooper would associate the park with the overzealous Doberman. Against my better judgment, I gave it another shot. With snow on the ground, maybe there would be light attendance. I was wrong. There were five other dogs racing around, mostly small mixed breeds. They all came rushing toward the fence. I let Cooper get acquainted through the chain link. There was plenty of tail wagging, so we ventured in. The people standing there urged me to take Cooper's leash off. I set him free. The other dogs immediately chased him down, with Cooper heading (with tail between his legs) straight back to the gate. I waited to see if he would settle in, but his next stop was at my feet, the pack circling around him. Then the frenzied dogs seemed to get annoyed with Cooper; he would not play. They relentlessly nipped at his hind legs. Suddenly one of the little buggers nailed me in the ankle. Ouch! Not a single owner stepped in to correct their dog. That was it! I quickly put Cooper's leash on and exited the dog park. Looking back, as I write this, I'm astonished that no one reacted. And there was silence as I left. It made me wonder if these people were not school-yard bullies in their youth. It will be a cold day in July before we revisit that facility. I may even write a letter to county officials that oversee the park. They need to separate dogs by size, just like other

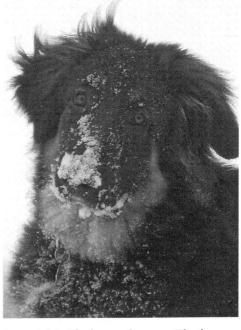

parks. For now, we'll just stick with doggy daycare. That's a controlled environment, not a free-for-all.

JANUARY 5

On more than one occasion, people have said, "Get Cooper's ears up!" Even Mom said, "They have to go up." But these are unusually large, floppy ears. And the vet wasn't hopeful that we would meet with success, citing the lack of cartilage. Nonetheless, we had to try, since they won't be going up on their own. I had to get the ball rolling, starting with an e-mail to Lynn ….

To: Lynn
From: D. Phillips

Happy New Year! I'm just touching base to see if you have time to set Cooper's ears this week, or whenever you think is best. Yesterday someone said, as you did, that they should be done soon, so I didn't want to procrastinate.

JANUARY 9

Unraveling toilet paper has become Cooper's favorite activity—when no one is looking. After finding mounds of paper on the bathroom floor, I've finally come to the conclusion that it's best to keep the door shut. Otherwise, I need to catch him in the act. Probably easier to keep the door shut.

JANUARY 10

I got Cooper's dog license from the town hall today. I learned the hard way what it can cost you dearly if you don't comply with the ordinance. During an unusually severe thunder storm, Sidney and Nicki (our goldens) bolted out of the pen, literally taking the gate off its hinges. A community resident, and one-time mayor, loaded the scared, soaking wet dogs into the back of his mini-van, and then off-loaded them at our back door. He demanded to know if the dogs were licensed. I said, "No." Back then, the last thing I worried about in our rural community was dog licenses. As long as all their vaccines were up to date, especially rabies, that's all I cared about. The very next day, the police appeared at our front door, with summons in hand. The whole fiasco set me back $300, and further solidified this man's reputation as the resident trouble-maker. Sure, he was enforcing the law, but who castigates a dog owner whose pets escaped during a storm? It was all in very bad form.

JANUARY 12

Cooper needed to see Dr. Reynolds for a routine checkup and Bordatella shot. It's first-come, first-served in the vet's office, so we signed in and waited. The room was packed with every type of dog imaginable, from a tiny puggle (pug and beagle mix) to a large collie. Cooper watched all of the commotion, but was unperturbed. He sat quietly as people traipsed in and out. An hour into our wait, when I really wished I had a book to read, our neighbor and his six-year-old son walked in. They came right up to say hello and meet the big dog. The little boy, John, stood just as high as Cooper, eye-to-eye. Since Cooper has had virtually no exposure to small children and our experience at Borders did replay in my mind; I kept watch for anything funny—but there was no reaction whatsoever. When we got into the examining room, Cooper was a bit nervous, but nothing out of the ordinary. Dr. Reynolds checked his heart, ears, teeth and gums. Next, the shot. He took that in stride as well. This vet visit—my first with Cooper—was a success.

January 14

Taking a walk was not on Cooper's list of favorite things to do today. When I led him out the side gate to the street, he promptly sat down in the driveway. He wouldn't move. He just looked up at me, as if to say, "I'm not ready for this." I relented, and took him back into the house. On this day, I would walk with only my iPod for company.

January 18

Cooper's big day! He gets his ears taped. John and I arrived at Valley Crest Kennel's grooming salon. Lynn loved seeing Cooper again. Jill came down shortly thereafter. The process of taping a German shepherd's ears is not for a beginner. It involved precise placement of a glue-covered foam curler within the ear, which is then bound by tape. To keep the ears in an upright position, tape is used to connect the two ears at the top of the head. Unlike Dobermans, and other breeds, there is nothing "surgical" about this procedure.

As Jill worked on Cooper, I could tell Lynn was happy to have the help. After a few attempts, Jill was pleased with the results. Cooper, however, was not so pleased. I tried to distract him with treats, but the smell of glue, the spongy curlers, and the surgical tape were not to his liking. Jill suggested keeping Cooper occupied when we got home, so he wouldn't try to scratch the tape and possibly damage his ears. So after the "operation," we took a stroll through town. That evening, Cooper was fine, just occasionally shaking his head. What I have to remember is to check his ears

every day for any signs of infection. That can be easily done by sniffing at the base of the ears. Jill left space for air flow, but infection is always possible.

JANUARY 19

Amy's compact car took a direct hit from an SUV. To my relief, her car was parked in a driveway; only the grill was damaged. Her friend's mother didn't see the car parked behind her. When Amy took the car for repair, Cooper went along for the ride. Everyone at the body shop was gaga over Cooper. The office manager said to Amy, in no uncertain terms, "The only way you can pick up the car is if you bring Cooper back." Now that is a dog-friendly workplace.

LESSONS LEARNED

✔ Taking a puppy into a busy store during the holidays might not be such a good idea. Cooper was clearly overwhelmed at Amy's place of work—wrong place, wrong time. We were cornered in the vestibule by throngs of shoppers and a well-intentioned, but overzealous, dog lover.

✔ A dog needs one or more forms of identification. This can include a microchip, license tag (proof that the dog is licensed in your town and inoculated against rabies) and name tag

> The ASPCA's Vice President of Shelter Research and Development, Dr. Emily Weiss, has confirmed through scientific research that simple pet ID tags can drastically increase the return to owner (RTO) rate.

(with phone number and address). Remember, not having a dog license can come back to bite you, since it is a law in many states.

✔ Dog parks aren't for everyone. If you go that route, watch what goes on before introducing your dog. If owners are more interested in talking to one another, rather than paying attention to their dog, I would stay away. Negative experiences at an early age can leave a lasting impression on a dog. Confirming that fact is an article titled *Raising a confident puppy* (*www.vonlotta.com/raising.html*). The writer recommends avoiding the company of adult dogs, specifically saying, "Do not take your pup to dog parks." Should the dog be attacked at a young age, often he will grow to be dog aggressive.

✔ A puppy should mingle with senior citizens and all of their assistive devices, like canes, walker and wheelchair. These things can spook a dog. In order to desensitize Cooper, I intentionally expose him to my mother's equipment. We're slowly making progress.

✔ It is not a foregone conclusion that a puppy will destroy your belongings. While our first goldens did major damage to the house and our belongings, Cooper hasn't shown a similar destructive streak. That may be the exception rather than the rule, and could certainly change as he gets older. As a precaution, Cooper is secured in his crate whenever we leave the house. The crate should be a "short-term confinement area," as it's called by Andrea Arden, expert dog trainer (*www.andreaarden.com*).

✔ The ears of a shepherd puppy may not go up on their own. That was a complete surprise to me. I had no idea that glue, curlers and tape would be required. To get a better idea of what we were facing, I Googled *German shepherd ear taping*.

Month 4: The Ear Saga Continues

"Since life and experience is a matter
of trial-and-error, there's no need to take
choosing—or life itself—too seriously."

—*Soren Lauritzen*

January 20, 2010

While getting Cooper's ears taped last week, we got the e-mail address for Pancho's owner. Since Pancho was our inspiration for getting a long-coat shepherd, I wanted to send him a few pictures of Cooper.

To: Michel
From: D. Phillips

We saw Jill at Valley Crest Kennels on Monday; she set Cooper's ears (pic attached), and she was kind enough to give me your e-mail. I've also included a puppy pic taken on the day we brought him home.

We've had Cooper just three months now and he is, by far, the smartest dog we've ever owned. We're working on his shyness with strangers, taking him all over town and through any business that won't object—Home Depot, the bank, pet stores, you name it. He's also completed Puppy Kindergarten and is headed to Level I Obedience, so we're hoping to have a well-adjusted companion dog.

And, thanks for sending a picture of Pancho. He's a very handsome dog!

JANUARY 25

Lynn was kind enough to inquire into the status of Cooper's ears. I explained that he was doing great. They are perfectly symmetrical and he does not pay any attention to the mass of material on his head. He is getting with the program and ready to go to Level I Obedience class on February 24. The only problem is, he cannot be around other dogs when his ears are taped. It is too dangerous, as another dog could bite his ears or get caught up in the tape, causing injury. So I asked if we could cut the tape between the ears and reattach it after the session. Lynn thought that would be okay—and it was.

FEBRUARY 11

I thought we might have success when we removed the tape from Cooper's ears, but they came down. One creased in the middle, the other pointed to the side; reminded me of Yoda from *Star Wars*. I asked Lynn if we should wait to see what happens naturally or retape the ears soon. I didn't want to lose any window of opportunity to get the ears up, as he is such a handsome dog with both up. Lynn said, "Let's put them right back up. They are big and I think they need more time in curlers." We set a date for retaping.

FEBRUARY 15

Jill retaped Cooper's ears. Having already experienced this process once, Cooper was not terribly cooperative. She and Lynn teamed up and got the job done. I really appreciated all of their effort. I just hope it's not in vain.

FEBRUARY 16

Cooper is exactly six months old today. To mark the occasion, we're going to let him have complete run of the house. He has been very reliable—house training was a breeze. And I'm still not seeing any signs that he'll turn his attention to eating the trim off the door frames. Skipper (our first golden) did just that, *and* ate a hole in the wall-to-wall carpet. That was before crates were in common use.

FEBRUARY 18

Going to the gas station is another opportunity to socialize Cooper; I put the back car window down just low enough so he can get his head through, but not so far that he could fit his body. Our usual stop, Exxon, has nice attendants that always have a biscuit at the ready. While Cooper does not take these treats, it is a friendly gesture. On this day, the attendant asked, "Is he friendly?" I said, "Yes." He extended his hand into the car to pet Cooper on the head, and then asked about his ears. I explained they were just taped to get them into proper position. He then said, "The last time I stuck my hand in a car a Rottweiler clamped down and wouldn't let go." After freeing his arm, all the young man remembered was the driver taking off at a high rate of speed.

LESSONS LEARNED

✔ A shepherd's ears should be up by the time he's done teething. This is typically between four and five months of age. If not, it's time to take action. But before undertaking this yourself, consult with your breeder and/or veterinarian. *Note*: Conventional wisdom is that if the puppy's ears on not standing by eight months of age, they are not going to.

✔ When ears are taped, there should be ample space left at the base of the ear. This allows for air flow, otherwise infection can set in. To check for any signs of bacteria build-up, I gave Cooper's ears a quick sniff once a day. No odor was ever detected.

✔ Never let a dog with taped ears play with other dogs, off-leash. There's a very real chance of injury.

✔ Ear tape may need to stay in place for weeks, and possibly be repeated. During these critical weeks of puppy development, it's important to continue socializing the dog.

✔ If a puppy appears frightened of people approaching the car, for instance, a gas station attendant, use your judgment about opening the window. To work through this, you might try giving the attendant the puppy's favorite treat. Hopefully, the puppy will take the bait.

MONTH 5: BAD DOG!

"Because no two dogs are alike,
a shy dog cannot be corrected the way
one would correct an aggressive dog."

—*Siegel & Margolis*

FEBRUARY 20

A trip to Walmart turned very scary. As Amy ran to the photo department, Cooper and I stood outside. A very busy place, Cooper could take in the sights—noisy carts, small children, all of the things that would potentially frighten a dog. As I was talking to two women, eager to pet Cooper, a Subaru wagon pulled up. What happened next caught me completely off guard. One of the women standing next to me was waiting for her husband to pick her up from work. The car was just a few feet away from us when she opened the passenger door. In a flash, a fawn-colored pit bull—muscle from head to toe—bolted from the front seat, *with* leash, *without* human. Running loose, the pit bull was lightning fast, jumping all over and around Cooper, who was frozen in place. As the scene unfolded, I wasn't sure if the dog was intending to inflict damage. In that split second, I feared the worst. Not helping matters, the woman was screaming at the top of her lungs. While she had grabbed the leash, she could not control the powerful dog. I was desperately trying to create space between the pit bull and Cooper, but it was impossible. The dog was too fast. Finally, the husband got out of the car. He forced the dog into the back seat, only to watch him jump right through the still-open front passenger-side door. Bolting right back at Cooper, Act II was underway. They did succeed in corralling the dog, but with great difficulty. As my heart was still racing, I thanked God that this pit bull, a much-maligned breed, was more curious than dangerous.

FEBRUARY 24

John took Cooper to Level I Obedience training with Cheryl. At this point, Cooper has all the basics down, so John felt the class was not challenging enough. On the one hand, I was delighted to hear that Cooper excelled, but waiting until the next class delays the interaction with other dogs, which is just as important as the training itself. I guess I could ignore

John's opinion and take Cooper next week, but I'll see when the Level II Obedience class is offered.

FEBRUARY 26

Cooper's ears are still holding, with tape removed. This leaves the curlers to do all of the work. I've got my fingers crossed that when the foam is removed that we'll have success.

FEBRUARY 28

Cooper and I were thrown out of Staples today. We had enjoyed two previous visits, without attracting attention, but on this day the manager rushed up to me and said, "Is that a service dog?" I responded, "He's in training." Apparently that doesn't cut it. I was asked to leave. Cooper sat in the car while I shopped.

MARCH 1

Cooper's favorite pastime is to chase his soccer and volleyball. I believe he is herding them into one corner of the pen. He grabs one and races over to the other. Since he can't hold two in his mouth at the same time, I throw the free ball. He never tires of this, which makes me think that herding training might be a great outlet. I asked Cheryl if she knew of any places that specialized in herding. She referred me to Raspberry Ridge Sheep Farm in Bangor, PA, where they conduct herding instinct tests, training seminars, and even aggression rehab classes.

MARCH 3

Bob and Susan brought Molly over for her first-ever playtime with Cooper. The fenced yard gave them just enough space to stretch their legs, mostly as Molly pursued Cooper; he loved it. But the chilly weather caused us to retreat to the house. The dogs continued their game of tag in the kitchen, while we talked about the dogs. I told them that I had invited a friend and neighbor, Jane, over to see how Cooper reacts to her at the door. I'm sensing that his instinct to protect is really kicking in. As if on cue, there was a knock at the door. Cooper had just collapsed in the kitchen, from sheer exhaustion. As I opened

the door to let Jane in, Cooper didn't even get up. There was no reaction at all. I had expected some response. This had gone swell. Jane wondered what I was worried about. Molly, on the other hand, was making up for Cooper's silence, barking directly at Jane. Bob tried to calm her, but she was intent on protecting the house, even if it wasn't hers.

MARCH 5

Today was not a good day. I was working in my office when I heard Cooper barking in the kitchen, directly below. This was no ordinary bark, but aggressive barking that grew steadily louder and louder. I ran downstairs to see what the commotion was all about. John was standing there with the plumber, Jim. As I entered the room, Cooper began to calm down. John then said, "Cooper nipped Jim." I said, "No way! He wouldn't do that," as if to convince myself. Jim said, "He nipped my arm, but only caught my sleeve," as he stretched his left arm toward me. While I was glad there was no "bite," the realization that Cooper made an aggressive move on a visitor was devastating. While my heart raced, I wanted to give John an ear full for not managing Cooper. I'm sure it all happened too fast, so I'm glad I held back. In hindsight, John should have had better control over the dog, so the two could get acquainted. But Cooper didn't appear in any mood to shake hands, and instead chose to snap, apparently in an attempt to guard his territory—the kitchen. Cooper has gotten into the habit of standing at the top of the basement stairs and barking at any non-family member emerging from the darkness. I had no experience with a protective dog. The goldens would bark, to alert you, but never nip anyone. This episode gave me real cause for concern.

MARCH 6

While I thought yesterday was bad, things would get far worse. My brother, Stuart, was coming over, but arrived early. Cooper was in the kitchen; I was in my office. Suddenly all hell broke loose. This time, I knew what was going on and high-tailed it downstairs. Stuart had a chair firmly planted between his body and Cooper; the dog was determined to keep him right there. With hackles up, the barking continued, even as I entered the room. Stuart yelled, "Cooper nipped my ass!" At this point, Cooper still had him pinned. I grabbed the dog by the scruff of the neck and squeezed hard, gave a quick shake, and said, "Bad dog!" Cooper backed off immediately, putting his head down, almost in shame. He got the message. Yesterday, with the plumber, the correction would have been too late; I needed to react immediately. Stuart emerged from behind the chair, visibly shaken. Everyone settled down; Stuart was not hurt. While Cooper did not draw any blood, he surely drew Stuart's ire; his opinion of Cooper had been forever changed. As Stuart got to the top of the basement steps, Cooper circled around behind him, and took a cheap shot, an ambush really. With a second vicious human-dog encounter, in as many days, it was painfully apparent that I've got a serious problem.

MARCH 7

After going through two consecutive days of Cooper acting badly, I couldn't sleep. I tossed and turned, thinking about what to do next. Should I give Cooper back to the breeder? How would Amy and John feel if they woke up tomorrow and Cooper was gone? I spent hours agonizing over the options. That morning, in my sleep-deprived state, just the sight of Amy brought me to tears. She was clearly uncomfortable with my emotional state; she tried her best to comfort me. Deep down, I'm sure she felt the same sense of dread. I really hadn't exercised due diligence in the puppy search process. I should have insisted on meeting the sire and dam. What type of temperament did those dogs have? I may never know because I didn't ask any questions. We brought a fearful puppy into our home, and now it was up to *me* to figure out the best course of action.

The only thing I could think to do was call Jill at Valley Crest Kennel. I wanted her advice on how to handle Cooper's bad behavior. I had also jotted down ways to broach the topic of taking Cooper back:

> *"I don't know if I have the ability to manage him and wanted to know if you and Lynn would take him back."*

> *"If we come to the decision that we cannot keep him, would you and Lynn take him back?"*

Once I had Jill on the phone, I didn't say anything about taking the dog back. Jill just urged me to seek professional help, saying "Cooper needs training," and "You must nip this in the bud right away." She then said, "Please let me know how you make out." Though not minimizing the seriousness of my situation, she still wasn't forthcoming with any advice. In fact, when I asked if she had ever encountered such a situation with one of her puppies, she had not. Yes, indeed, this was the first time in decades of breeding shepherds that one of her puppies was out of line. This was preposterous, but I didn't press her any further. Instead, I agreed to let her know what happens. She wanted to be able to "help other people," if she ever gets a similar call. Like a witness under cross examination, I could tell I wasn't going to extract any nuggets of knowledge on how to remedy our (my) problem. Instead, after hanging up the phone, I was left asking myself, "What do I do now?" "How did we get to this place?" Our mild-mannered puppy turned on two people, in as many days. The foreboding of what our future held was overwhelming. We had shown Cooper nothing but love and affection. Perhaps that had to change, by showing him that *we* are the pack leaders. Only one problem, I didn't know how.

MARCH 8

Good news and bad news today. Good news: Cooper's ears appear to be staying up. We took the tape off. So far, so good. He looks so much better now. Bad news: I still need to address Cooper's poor greeting behavior, so I e-mailed Lynn.

To: Lynn
From: D. Phillips

I talked to Jill yesterday, concerned about Cooper's nipping people that come into the house. It's not vicious or anything, just barking and a quick nip. He got my

brother's backside this weekend. What is your opinion,
besides correcting him with a stern "No?" We give
visitors biscuits to distract him, but he's instinctively
guarding his domain. Jill said to get him to training. He
went to Level I Obedience, but he knew everything, so
he is enrolled in Level II Obedience. Like Jill said, we
need to nip this in the bud. Otherwise, he is okay when
we are out and about. It's just in the house. Since we're
new to the breed, any advice would be much appreciated.
Thanks!

I received a short e-mail message from Lynn, who was not
pleased to hear about Cooper's bad manners. She wanted me to
stay on top of him, but said that she would get back to me with
more guidance after talking to Jill.

I also left a message for Cheryl, which she returned while
I was on my way to doggy daycare. Cooper was in need of
playtime. To avoid talking on my cell while driving, I pulled
into a garden center parking lot. Cheryl and I talked at great
length. With decades in the dog training business, she was
very familiar with shepherds. She felt that Cooper "took a
cheap shot" at my brother, by circling around behind him,
and punctuating his displeasure with a nip. I told her about a
facility that would train Cooper away from home. Another idea
was to return Cooper to the breeder. The first boot camp option
had me worried that Cooper would be beaten into submission,
and the thought of returning him to the breeder had me in
tears.

MARCH 8

While I waited to hear back from Lynn, I e-mailed the dog training facility that I mentioned to Cheryl. They came highly recommended by family friends. What's more, they train Doberman pinschers and German shepherds for the New Jersey State Police. To learn more about their program, I reached out via e-mail:

To: SJ Kennel
From: D. Phillips

We're owners of a six-month-old German shepherd. He's highly intelligent and a great family pet. However, as a new puppy, he was shy and fearful of people. We take him everywhere and introduce him to sights and sounds, which has helped. He passed Puppy Kindergarten with flying colors, though he did not interact with other dogs during the play session. In public, he alternates between sniffing strangers and backing off when they approach. With other dogs, he's indifferent or curious, never aggressive.

Our problem is when he's in the kitchen, the main living area of our house. His greeting behavior has gone from barking to two recent nipping events. He was not vicious, just defending his territory, as I was not there to reassure him that "It's okay."

While we like having a protective dog that alerts us when someone comes over, I cannot live with one that may one day bite. So, my question... Is it possible to correct this type of behavior after your two-week on-site training? The trainer said we should either give him back to the breeder or manage him on a daily basis. We're very attached at this point, and so we'd like to think he can be trained to avoid any escalation in aggression. He's received nothing but positive training and love since we got him at eight weeks, so I can't help but think he's got the right foundation to lead a good life.

If he were a training candidate at your facility, what is the fee and when could we start?

MARCH 9

In response to my e-mail, I received a call from the training facility. We set up a time for the trainer, the son of the kennel owner, to come evaluate Cooper and take him back to their kennel. Since Cooper was being neutered the next day, we needed to hold off on that meeting.

MARCH 10

The day of reckoning—Cooper's surgery. With his bad manners, being neutered could help with a much-needed attitude adjustment. I was pleased that Robert, Dr. Reynolds' knowledgeable longtime office manager, was working. He pointed out that there are no guarantees that the operation will temper Cooper's wild side. However, it is the responsible thing to do. He is just a pet, so keeping him intact would be pointless. Robert then asked me to leave first, so he could more easily coax Cooper into the back room.

I picked Cooper up later in the day, a bit groggy but otherwise none the worse for wear. To prevent him from biting the stitches, he had been fitted with an Elizabethan collar. Surely uncomfortable for Cooper, it was just as much a nuisance for us since we have to remove the collar to allow Cooper to eat and drink. Being the geniuses we are, it was a struggle figuring out how to put it back on.

MARCH 11

Lynn got back to me with feedback from Valley Crest's owner about Cooper's bad behavior. We were thinking along the same lines, as she and Jill suggested professional intervention. I explained that I had already reached out to a dog training facility. She also wanted me to watch a training video called *Calming Signals: What does your dog tell you?* I promised to stop by the kennel. I'll try anything at this point.

E-mailed Cheryl; she was so helpful when Cooper's nipping incidents first occurred, giving me much-needed guidance on possible steps to take.

To: Cheryl
From: D. Phillips

Thanks for your advice on how to tackle Cooper's greeting behavior. We've decided to send him to a two-week obedience class at a professional dog training facility. A friend of ours had great results with their dog. The trainer also works with us here at the house to reinforce the training.

While I briefly considered asking the breeder to take him back, we've gotten so attached that we first have to give Cooper a chance. As Robert at Dr. Reynolds' office said, "You don't give up your kid because he misbehaved." Of course, if the professional training doesn't work, we'll have other more serious decisions to make, but I'm going to remain positive.

So our first step was to have Cooper neutered, which was done yesterday. Robert thought we were taking the correct action by neutering him and two weeks later starting intensive training. Cooper is so naturally obedient that I think once he knows what is and isn't acceptable behavior, we'll have a great pet.

MARCH 12

Cheryl inquired about Cooper today, which was really very nice, and answered an earlier question about herding training. Cooper, like all shepherds, needs a job, so this might be just the ticket. She also said something about the breed that was interesting: German shepherds are livestock-guarding dogs—a living fence as it were—not so much a gathering breed like border collies.

MARCH 18

Cesar Millan, the *Dog Whisperer*, advocates exercise, discipline, and then affection. To heed those words, I've let Cooper join John on his slow jogs down the street, a one-mile round trip. Though I know that Cooper should be older before running, I cannot bring myself to tell John to wait. This is a new, healthy activity for both of them, so I want to be supportive. I just hope that this early exercise regimen doesn't do any permanent damage. Besides, how would sheep farmers in Germany keep puppies from running through the countryside? They wouldn't. Perhaps the issue is more a matter of young dogs running on hard surfaces, like macadam. Repeated impact on a developing puppy's joints can't be good.

LESSONS LEARNED

- When in public, if a puppy tries to hide behind you, there are fear issues which can be an early sign of possible behavioral problems. Don't stop exposing the dog to new people and places. Over time, the puppy will learn that people are good.

- Neuter or spay your dog at six months of age. For pet owners, this is the responsible thing to do. However, as we were told, there is no guarantee that neutering or spaying will put an end to aggressive behavior. For more information, including low cost or free neuter/spay programs, visit *www.spayusa.com.*

- Challenge your dog by enrolling him in more advanced obedience classes. With their keen intelligence, German shepherd puppies excel; they are driven to please their owners.

- If a puppy is behaving badly, correction must be immediate. Even five seconds after a deed is done is too late. And when we catch Cooper in the act, he is never hit, yelled at or beaten. When Cooper nipped my brother, I grabbed the scruff of his neck, mimicking the guiding bite of an alpha dog, as I said, "Bad dog!" He got the message. Nothing more was necessary. Maintaining an even keel will help the puppy, being raised as a family pet, to develop an even temper, that is, one not prone to ferocious outbursts.

✓ Keep a supply of dog treats in your pocket. Whether to reinforce good behavior in the house or to allow people to feed the puppy in public. The dog will realize that good things happen when people approach. Note that some people are against this practice; I see no harm.

✓ When out with your dog, be prepared for the unexpected. That includes sudden encounters with other dogs. Our experience with the loose pit bull at Walmart underscored how things can go from calm to calamity in mere seconds.

> Puppies are not unlike their human counterparts, babies, with all the demands they entail. So you must be committed to taking an active role in the dog's development, inside and outside of the home.

✓ German shepherds are guard dogs. Even if raised with kindness, like Cooper, the dog can still exhibit protective behavior, particularly in the house. Ian Dunbar's book titled *The Essential German Shepherd Dog*, says, "When there is no flock to protect, the German shepherd protects his people and their property." He goes on to say, "This protective instinct is what makes the breed valuable to the police and military. Because of this instinct, German shepherds do not greet every person they meet with a wagging tail and a licking tongue." My brother would surely agree.

✔ If you don't know a dog, don't let the dog get behind you. As I've watched Cooper, he circles around visitors, again an instinct maneuver, so a nip could be in the offing.

✔ To learn which dog breeds are most protective, visit *www. petmedsonline.org/top-10-best-guard-dog-breeds.html*.

✔ If unacceptable behavior surfaces in a puppy, take action right away. Letting a nip here or there slide is a recipe for disaster. Consult with your breeder, veterinarian and local dog trainers. There are so many resources available, including trainers that specialize in shepherds.

✔ Heed Cesar Millan's words—exercise, discipline, affection. All dogs, not just shepherds, need to be active. Engage your dog in activities that stimulate his mind and body. For more information on Cesar's training tips and information resources, visit *www.cesarsway.com*.

✔ One way to challenge your shepherd is through herding classes. Check for any facilities in your area that might offer this activity. I was referred to Raspberry Ridge Sheep Farm in Bangor, PA. For more information, visit *www. raspberryridgesheepfarm.com*.

MONTH 6: DON'T GIVE UP ON THAT DOG!

"If you have built castles in the air, your work need not be lost. This is where they should be. Now, put the foundation under them."

—*Henry David Thoreau*

MARCH 21

Amy said something today that had me questioning my decision to get a shepherd. She said, "My friends are too afraid to come over." Centrally located in the county, Amy's high school and college friends can easily meet here before a night out. The "open door" policy, however, no longer exists. Precautions must be taken. With Cooper's protective instinct, he can be quite imposing at the door. Amy knows the drill. She gives visitors biscuits to offer Cooper, which soothes his ruffled feathers. But some people are so frightened that they toss the treats on the floor, directing Cooper away from them. While this does focus Cooper's energy elsewhere, it just can't be a long-term solution.

As I continue to anguish over the dog, John and Amy are preoccupied with work and school. Perhaps if my office were outside the home, I too would see things differently. Instead, I feel as if I'm in the eye of a storm, with no knowledge of its direction or intensity. The feelings of dread remind me of a past pet debacle, Amy's ferret. Unlike Cooper, that silly, smelly critter was innocuous.

MARCH 22

The dog training facility was scheduled to pick Cooper up at 12:00 p.m. today. Noon came and went. When I tried to reach my contact, strange events unfolded. It involved the office manager and the facility owner's son. Since he failed to bring his client (Cooper) back, I suspect he will be in hot water. In fact, with the bizarre conversations I had with this young man, it gave me pause to reconsider my decision to send Cooper away. The office manager was very apologetic, but I canceled the off-site training. There must be a better way. In the meantime, I scheduled Cooper for local training, and took that opportunity to ask Cheryl about underground fences and electronic collars (also called e-collars).

From: D. Phillips
To: Cheryl

Pencil us in for Level II Obedience on May 18. I'd really like to see how Cooper does. On another note, what do you think of electronic collars and invisible fences? I know people that use one or the other. I'm just not sure how a GSD would typically handle either.

Cheryl didn't feel that an invisible fence is appropriate for any dog with aggressive tendencies; the dog can associate the pain with a dog/person walking by. You also have to remember that people coming to the house don't know where the line is. And as for e-collars, she would never advocate using pain to combat aggressiveness.

Cheryl made a lot of sense. My initial thinking was that an e-collar could substitute for an invisible fence. But since we walk Cooper every day, where he often encounters other dogs and people, I'm not getting a sense that he's at all aggressive. It's more curious/cautious. Would he make a move at someone walking by the house? We don't know, but we have a pen where he stays on nice days, and unlike our past golden retrievers, he doesn't bark at every moving object.

But while corresponding with Cheryl, I continued to question my decision to send Cooper away to doggy boot camp. John and Amy opposed the idea. Cooper is a very sensitive dog, so we may get back an entirely different dog. And in my soul searching, I once again reached out to Cheryl.

From: D. Phillips
To: Cheryl

I had Cooper at doggy daycare today and I talked at length with the owner. She sensed my trepidation about leaving Cooper at a training facility for two weeks. Maybe the best move is to have you work with us on the primary issue—greeting people at home. If he goes to dog boot camp, he may come back responding faster to commands, but you can't replicate what's happening in a home setting. The obedience stuff we can reinforce in your class in May. What are your thoughts?

Cheryl agreed with me about leaving Cooper at a training facility. Though they may be reputable, unless you're with the dog you don't know the methods they are using. Since she does not do one-on-one training, she suggested that I call a trainer who comes highly recommended, Steve LaVallee. If he has to come to the house once or twice, it will be a lot cheaper than sending Cooper away.

MARCH 23

I did as Cheryl suggested and visited Steve's website (*www.realk9solutions.com*). His experience was very impressive—a former Seeing Eye dog instructor, pilot dog instructor and dog trainer for the U.S. Marines. And as a Schutzhund* trainer and competitor, he had placed in a number of regional and national events. His website also indicates that he has trained dogs for television and movies. Steve works in your home, with the dog and the owner. Surely, I need training as much as Cooper. I need to be giving Cooper clear, consistent commands. I gave Steve a call and we're all set for a meeting on the 27th.

*Schutzhund means "Protection dog" in German.

MARCH 25

While still in a distressed state over Cooper's nipping incidents, I ran into a well-dressed gentleman at doggy daycare. As I waited to pay, he looked at Cooper and said, "What a gorgeous dog!" I quietly said, "We're having some issues. He's behaving badly when people come over." Saying those words, even to a complete stranger, had me on the verge of tears. His next statement stayed with me all day, and well beyond. He said, "Don't give up on that dog! If he's a jerk after a year and a half, two years, maybe then." He handed me his business card (which I cannot find) and left. He was so passionate in his plea, I took those few words very much to heart.

As I drove home with Cooper, a long-ago memory came flooding back. Shortly after John and I met in 1975, we were visiting his cousin's farm in eastern Pennsylvania. Having made the trip for a backyard barbeque, low and behold, they had a litter of yellow Labrador puppies. Needless to say, we ended up bringing home the most adorable puppy. We named her Brandy. John built her the Taj Mahal of dog houses, complete with a sliding Plexiglas window. Never mind that it weighed 500 pounds, it was so much fun to see John enjoying the dog. Reality, however, soon set in. We were far too busy to dedicate time to training a puppy. I was in college and John was working full time for his father in the painting business. Brandy occupied her time by peeling up the linoleum flooring in our kitchen. My mother was soon at the breaking point. The last straw was when she got a call from the police. Brandy had killed three ducks at the park. When I went to retrieve the dog, the police had placed her in a jail cell. There was something comical about that scene, but nothing funny about bringing her back home. For my mother, it was "Me or the dog," so John grudgingly agreed to take her back to his cousin's farm. We *did* give up on that dog, something I've regretted ever since. Years later, we heard that she had been killed by a hunter, possibly mistaken for a whitetail deer.

MARCH 26

Oh boy, Cooper's ear taping didn't hold. After I removed some sticky residue from his left ear, down it came. Amy thinks it's kind of cute, the floppy ear. Who knew we would even have to face such an issue. I was not at all happy. Maybe it was the sense of failure after so much time and energy was expended.

Thankfully, Jill and Lynn were kind enough to help us, yet again. Today, Jill chose to glue a photograph into Cooper's ear, a

picture of his daddy. She trimmed it until it fit nicely into the stubborn left ear. That seemed to do the trick. Only one problem: we keep looking down at Cooper and asking, "Who's your daddy?"

MARCH 27

Cooper's first home training session with Steve took place today. He began by working on Cooper's greeting behavior, coming to the front door without knocking. On this first try, he just greeted me verbally. Cooper approached the door. Steve asked that I move Cooper back. He then entered the living room. Cooper growled, a muffled growl, and was corrected, as his prong collar and leash were in place. I gave it a quick tug, and said, "No!" Steve, as he approached Cooper, gave him bits of hotdog, while I said, "It's okay." Cooper approached with his neck stretched out, very hesitant, but took the bait. I placed Cooper back at my side, in a sit position. We repeated this at the basement door, more of a trigger point. Cooper did not bark; Ozzie did all of the barking. We went through the same controlled introduction and treat process. Again, no barking on Steve's third entry into the basement stairwell.

Once there was no real fuss at either entry point, Steve moved to basic obedience training with sit and down commands. He used the leash very effectivexly to encourage compliance; when saying, "Down," he placed his foot on the leash and gently applied downward pressure. When asking Cooper to "Sit," he drew him into position with both the leash and treat. He repeated this sequence a number of times. Cooper caught on quickly. When the leash was handed to me, I worked on saying a command once and expecting Cooper to respond. Too often, I would say "Sit," "Sit," "Sit," where I was quickly reprimanded. "Say 'Sit' just once," Steve insisted.

Overall, this first session went very well, no barking, a slight growl—no signs of overt aggression. Steve felt that on a scale of 1 to 10, 10 being the most aggressive, Cooper was a 5, not so much for any outward signs of being a dangerous animal, just for Cooper's apparent shyness and fearful behavior (which can lead to aggression). That's why Steve is here—to prevent any escalation in fear on Cooper's part. My job is to be the pack leader and not allow Cooper to be the first to the door. If he is, I must step up, put Cooper in this place… basically saying, "I've got it. There's no need for you to make a fuss." In fact, Steve said there is no reason why Cooper should bark at all. That confused me. Don't you want your dog to alert when someone is at the door? He believes that can only lead to aggression. What's more, to paraphrase Steve, "Cooper will never take a bullet for you. If someone comes through that window, Cooper won't be any help."

After Steve left, Cooper and I continued our training with a trip to Main Street, taking along hotdog bits as rewards for good behavior. I needed a birthday card, so we headed to the pet store, an upscale establishment in the middle of town, which also carries hilarious pet-themed cards. Cooper has visited this shop since he was eight weeks old. But he is never entirely comfortable, perhaps since he draws so much patron attention. So as I strolled through the store, I periodically stopped to slip Cooper greasy hotdog bits. At one point, a tiny puppy emerged from around a corner. Cooper is so gentle with headstrong Ozzie that he knew to tread lightly with little dogs. Not only is Cooper good with other dogs, I've not seen any signs of food aggression. Another good sign, the clerk offered Cooper water and a treat, which he accepted, an indication he is beginning to relax.

Leaving the store, and only steps away, Cooper locked eyes on an approaching family. His pace slowed. I could immediately tell that the folks were delighted to see him, though I'm not sure the feeling was mutual. A woman, husband and teenage daughter stopped to greet Cooper. All was fine, as I handed everyone hotdog bits. Cooper was far more interested in engaging with strangers this time—thanks to the mystery meat.

As we headed back to the car, Cooper stepped up the pace—like a horse returning to the barn. I had to correct him with quick tugs on the leash; it was still a struggle. I tried reversing direction, to throw Cooper off course; it was to no avail. This is clearly an area we need to work on.

Cooper is exhausted. In just one day, he tolerated resetting of his floppy ear, an intensive training session with Steve, and a successful socialization session in town.

APRIL 1

Steve returned for another home training session with Cooper. We practiced proper greeting behavior; I placed Cooper behind me, in a subordinate position, as Steve entered the room. Steve is always prepared with an ample supply of hotdogs, so Cooper's more than willing to follow his lead. He noted how I'm not firm with my commands, and often repeat myself with "Sit," "Sit," "Sit!" Guilty!

Since Cooper understands the basic sit and down commands, we practiced "Go to bed." This command tells Cooper to go into his crate. Steve started by baiting the crate with hotdogs, as Cooper watched. He then led Cooper to the other side of the kitchen and, while releasing him, said, "Go to bed." Cooper didn't walk, he ran to the crate, where he was rewarded again, and Steve told him, "Down." I did the same thing. Same results. Cooper will cooperate when hotdogs are involved. The trick will be to get him to go to bed when someone is knocking at the door. That will be a sight to behold. Steve also believes in keeping the dog hungry, so he is food motivated, and suggests reducing his food supply. Not so sure about that.

Before leaving, Steve introduced Cooper to his own female German shepherd, Hasko, a small and very obedient dog indeed. Steve ran her through a few exercises in the driveway, which were impressive—particularly when she dropped to the ground, when being given the German command, *platz*.

APRIL 3

It was Easter weekend and I couldn't wait to see how Cooper would behave as family arrived. Stuart had called last night to warn that he would be entering the house with a stick in his hand, while ranting, "Why did you ever get that dog? He's a four-legged lawsuit." I assured him that if he carried a stick into the house, he would never be welcomed back. That shut him up.

Stuart arrived at 11:00 a.m. Since I had expected him later, Cooper was still in the pen, soaking up the sun's rays. As Stu entered the kitchen, he said, "Where's the dog?" I told him he was outside. He had walked right past Cooper, without the dog making a sound.

Well, I needed to conduct an experiment, so I asked Stu to go out the front door. I quickly ran out the back door to retrieve Cooper. From the kitchen, as I held on to Cooper, I yelled for Stu to knock on the front door. Cooper did not react. Stu came in the door, as I had Cooper leashed and slightly behind me, giving both Stu and Cooper plenty of space. Stu tossed hotdog bits to the floor. That was it; nothing to worry about. Apparently, hotdogs are a peace offering that Cooper can't resist. So with the nipping incident in the past, I'm hoping we can move forward… but Greg was expected shortly. Would that greeting go as well?

A few hours later, Gregory arrived by motorcycle. As he pulled into the garage, I could feel the house shake. I slipped downstairs to hand Greg a hotdog. We then repeated the same process, with Cooper on his leash, only this greeting was outside. Cooper was curious, but not threatening in any way. Throughout the weekend, Stu and Greg tossed biscuits to

Cooper. They became Cooper's best buddies. Cooper began engaging both of them in games of fetch, or more aptly called keep-away.

APRIL 4

This morning, Greg emerged from the guestroom armed with a handful of biscuits. Since Cooper was not accustomed to anyone other than us coming into the kitchen at that hour, we were taking no chances. And when my father-in-law, Al, arrived for Easter dinner, Cooper was once again outside. When Al approached the pen, Cooper growled, but otherwise made no fuss. Next time, I'll have Al greet Cooper with hotdogs; they'll be fast friends.

With Cooper's apparent good behavior, I let my guard down. Everyone had gathered in the yard for the annual golf-ball driving challenge. The property sits on the side of a hill, so smacking discarded range balls into the woods has been an annual event for over thirty years. As we all sat around, I allowed Cooper to run loose, which was a mistake. At 7-1/2 months, he is not likely to come when he's told. But since he seemed content to bounce about in front of the chicken coop, chasing the rooster and hens, I lost my focus. The chicken coop is very close to the road. Suddenly, Cooper and I saw the same thing, at exactly the same time—a bicyclist coming up the road.

My first thought: Cooper was too far away from me to grab him by the collar. Besides, he is unlikely to run *toward* a person. I was wrong. Cooper bolted into the street, barking a very scary bark. The instant the cyclist spotted Cooper, he stopped in his tracks, which was the right decision, as dogs see moving objects as prey. At the same time, I'm in pursuit and in a semi-panicked state. This man was distraught, coming face to face with a German shepherd. Cooper circled around him, extending his neck toward the rear wheel and growling. Was he going to bite the wheel or the cyclist's leg? I tried to remain calm, telling the man, "He's a puppy in training," while also firmly saying, "Cooper, no!" "Bad dog!" I literally chased him up the street, yelling "Bad dog!" until he made a quick left turn into our driveway. I secured him in the house. As a sensitive dog, which is how Steve describes him, Cooper got the message; he knew he had done something very wrong. Shortly thereafter, I put Cooper on his leash and we rejoined the party.

APRIL 5

Steve was back from his vacation, so we scheduled our third training session this afternoon, a jaunt through busy shopping areas in Flemington. We met up outside of a convenience store, a crowded setting that will give Steve an idea of how Cooper handles himself in public. Before heading out, I told him how good Cooper was over the weekend, his indoor greeting that is. We then walked the length of the strip mall and down a side street, Cooper pulling all of the way. Steve showed me how to give quick corrections when Cooper pulled, but I struggled. We crossed over into the ShopRite parking lot, where Steve said to not let people greet the cute dog with the fluffy coat, which seems to be quite a draw. I had to tell anyone who approached, "He's in training." This seemed to work, even as we sat on a bench, with Cooper lying at my side. As always, Cooper is a head-turner, but we completed our exercises without incident. When we returned to our cars, Steve introduced his black pug to Cooper. It was an adorable dog that Cooper gently sniffed. From his own little dog—Ozzie—at home, Cooper knew to be a tad wary of little dogs, which can have big attitudes. We then scheduled our last training session to take place at my home, so John and Amy could attend. I wanted the family in on this session, so we're all on the same page.

APRIL 6

We visited Cooper's breeder for a fourth taping of Cooper's left ear; the photo didn't hold. This time, Jill glued a curler into the ear and secured it in place with surgical tape. I thanked

both Jill and Lynn for "sticking" with me on what could be a losing battle. I also took the opportunity to tell Jill that I found a professional dog trainer for Cooper, to work on aggression issues. Her response was identical to when she and I first spoke about the problem. Having never seen this before in one of her

dogs, she once again urged me to let her know how I make out. With my journal in book form, she can learn exactly what I did.

APRIL 7

Two interesting comments from a neighbor I spoke with today. I asked her why she had German shepherds. This question originated from my own soul searching. Why did I get a shepherd? She answered without hesitation, "A good offense is the best defense." In our rural area, having a dog on the property can be an effective deterrent from unwelcome visitors. While we talked about socialization of her one-year-old female shepherd, she also told me that baby strollers scare the dog. She suggested that it's best to swing around the stroller, rather than approach straight on. Sounds like good advice.

APRIL 11

Another spin through Tractor Supply today. The employees are so nice to Cooper, always ready with a treat; Cooper has yet to accept. There are many sights, sounds and smells in the store, which makes it a perfect place to socialize a dog. Cooper is even learning to walk nicely beside the grocery cart, as we load up on puppy kibble and chicken feed. Janice, the store manager, has two Australian shepherds, so she is always kind, encouraging Cooper to take a biscuit, but no go. We'll keep at it.

APRIL 12

I have made a mistake. Since Cooper entered our home, nighttime has been playtime. In hindsight, I should have made daytime playtime. Unfortunately, the pattern is well established. After dinner is finished, and we retire to the living room, to read and watch television, Cooper kicks into high gear. This does not impact John, as he typically ignores Cooper's attempts to play, so I've become #1 playmate. I wonder if getting another shepherd would entertain him, but that is only a fleeting thought. The nighttime ritual includes training, tricks, and then play. We work on sit, down and stay. We then move to "Go in circles," "Bang!" (play dead) and "Which hand?" In all, he must have a dozen tricks under his collar. After reinforcing basic obedience, Cooper grabs one of his many rope toys, violently swinging it from side-to-side, as if it were a squirrel. After tiring of that, he then drops it at my feet. I toss the rope into the kitchen. Back and forth we go, for at least an hour. By 9:00 p.m., Cooper is usually exhausted, as am I.

APRIL 17

Over the past few months, I have found five of Cooper's teeth on the floor. A few others I have found dangling in his mouth, so I helped the process along. Only once was it a bloody affair. Looking back, I don't remember ever seeing a single golden's tooth, loose or otherwise. Perhaps this is due to Cooper having the largest set of canine choppers I've ever seen; even the baby teeth were remarkably large. I've collected them in a baggie, just like I did with Amy's teeth. Maybe I've gone too far.

LESSONS LEARNED

✔ Not everyone loves dogs, so be prepared to give those people space. German shepherds, in particular, can sense a person's fear, which can make matters worse.

✔ Visitors shouldn't look directly at your dog, which he can interpret as confrontational. Extending a hand, palm down, can allow the dog to get familiar with their scent. In addition to avoiding eye contact, Cesar Millan also stresses that people should not talk to or touch the dog; the dog should approach them, not the other way around.

✔ An off-site training facility may not be right for some dogs. A two-week stay away from our home wasn't the answer for Cooper. He's too sensitive to correction. Placing him in doggy boot camp, with unknown training methods, could have left us with an entirely different dog. Though I had heard favorable reviews about the training of an overly exuberant Labrador, I had serious doubts that strategy would work for a shy dog. The authors of *Good Dog, Bad Dog*, Siegal and Morgolis, say that shy dogs need "...compassion, patience, and a more methodical approach to dog training. You must not be overbearing...."

✔ In-home dog training is an excellent way to correct behavioral issues that are triggered in that setting. I learned that by placing Cooper in a subordinate position, behind me, I could stop his barking as people came up the basement stairs. The alternative would be to place him in a crate whenever anyone came over. In my eyes, that strategy would not address the problem. I may have felt differently about the crate if Cooper was considered dangerous.

✔ Hard biscuits may not do the trick when you want to reward the dog or encourage a shy puppy to take a treat from a stranger. So find a treat that the dog can't refuse, like hotdogs or any soft training treat.

✔ Letting a German shepherd run loose in your yard is not a good idea. Cooper unexpectedly darted into the street to investigate a bicyclist. We'll stick to the fenced portion of the yard from now on.

> If you consult a dog trainer, be honest about your dog's behavior. Some may say that full disclosure prejudices the trainer against the dog, but by holding any information back you place the trainer in possible danger.

✔ If you are having trouble with a dog, heed a wise man's words, "Don't give up on that dog." Bringing a dog into your home is a huge commitment. And if problems develop, they can likely be traced back to the owner. With Cooper, I wasn't stepping up to the plate. Once I learn the correct methods from a professional trainer who had the needed objectivity, we were on the right path. Cooper's behavior was markedly better.

✔ Invisible fences are not recommended for dogs with aggressive tendencies. And from what I'm told by friends and family who have installed these fences, they are far from foolproof. A break in the line can go undetected, allowing the dog to roam free and a headstrong dog will disregard the electric shock and bolt. As for e-collars, those are best left to the professionals.

✔ Daily playtime—which is necessary for all puppies— should fit your schedule. I made the mistake of engaging with Cooper after dinner. It's now an ingrained behavior...

when I sit down to watch read or watch television, Cooper appears with a ball in his mouth. He's so eager to play, I can't refuse.

Month 7:
A Near Tragedy

**"He who learns but does not think, is lost!
He who thinks but does not learn
is in great danger."**

—Confucius

May 1

Cooper has been perfecting a new trick over the last few months, "Get the paper." Since Stuart's Labrador revels in this job, I thought Cooper would as well. Each morning, Cooper follows me out to the driveway. I keep an eye out for cars, joggers, walkers, and the like, since he could dash into the road. When the coast is clear, I say, "Get the paper!" There's only one problem, once he picks the paper up and races back to the house, the paper invariably lands right outside the door. If I run ahead and open the door, it's a perfect operation, as he lets go inside, when I say, "Drop it!" I just need to work on slowing him down, and focus his attention away from tearing the plastic wrapper to shreds.

May 3

Cheryl was kind enough to ask how Cooper was doing with his home training, so I sent a message off to her...

To: Cheryl
From: D. Phillips

Cooper is doing great! We've had three sessions with Steve. Our last was to be yesterday, but he had to reschedule. I wanted one session with the family, so they get on board. I would say that getting Cooper neutered was the first step. Almost immediately, I sensed a difference. There's no more barking at guests. He's really quite mellow. He's still not fond of people making a fuss over him when we walk through town, but when Steve and I took him around ShopRite in Flemington, he tolerated the chaos well. There's no sign of aggression towards people or dogs. So I'm looking forward to the next stage in his training. Steve has helped us reinforce the basics and now we'll see how he does in a group setting. Thanks for touching base!

MAY 6

For the second time in just one month, I made a critical mistake while pulling the car into the garage. I left the car in drive, and then turned the engine off. The first time this happened, my memory lapse caused the car to come to rest against the closed garage door. If not for the door, the car would have careened down the hill, directly into the barn. You would have thought I had learned my lesson. Apparently not. This second episode was far more frightening.

I had just returned home, with the newly-groomed Ozzie sitting in the front seat, and Cooper in the back seat. Pulling into the garage, I pressed the interior garage door button—

the one attached to my rearview mirror, closing the door. This maneuver allows me to let Cooper out of the back seat, without him running away. But on this occasion, I was juggling multiple tasks. Ozzie had jumped on my lap, anxious to get out. Not thinking, I once again left the car in drive and turned the engine off.

With Ozzie safely in my arms, I let Cooper out the driver's side back seat. I cleared the back of the car and was headed toward the basement door when, in my periphery, I saw the car moving backward. As I swung around, with Ozzie still in my arms, I heard a wheezing sound. I looked down to see Cooper's body lodged between the back bumper and the garage door. I dropped Ozzie to the concrete floor, as gently as I could, and ran to the garage door opener. In an adrenalin rush, I did the worst thing possible—hit the button. I thought this would release Cooper from a death grip. As the door moved upward, the metal handle reached Cooper's rib cage, slowly pulling him skyward. Terrified, all I could do was wedge my body between the garage door and bumper, pushing the car forward with all my might. Suddenly, the door stopped. The door sensor had actually done its job, allowing me to release the pressure on Cooper. He slowly backed away from me; he was free.

At this point I didn't know if Cooper was injured. He and Ozzie were running around the garage, as I was holding the car from rolling backward; I was in a real fix. I had my cell phone, but no one to call. My husband and daughter were at work. What do I do now? Again, another stupid thought enters my mind. Toss something at that garage door button, only six feet away. I feared that letting the car go would ruin the partially-opened door. In hindsight, who cares about the garage door at a time like this? Instead, I held the car in place with my body.

As the seconds ticked away, I spotted two 10-pound dumbbells. They were within reach! I grabbed one and tossed it under the passenger-side tire, extending my foot to secure it tightly against the tire. It worked! I raced around the front of the car, jumped in, and shifted into park. After securing the car, I called to Cooper. Feeling his ribs and legs, he was fine—no broken bones or abrasions. I, on the other hand, was seriously shaken by my stupidity.

Later, Mom asked a good question: "Why does a car that is turned off roll, as if in neutral?" I called the car dealership and explained what happened. I left out the part about the dog nearly dying. The technician I spoke with was not surprised by the incident. He said, "It happens all of the time." He suggested always using the parking brake, which I never do. When I do engage the brake, I invariably drive off with it still engaged. However, after this experience, I will never turn the car off while still in drive. And I will always use the parking brake. Tragedy averted. Lesson learned.

MAY 8

My brothers visited for Mother's Day. When I recounted my harrowing experience with Cooper getting wedged between the car and garage door, Greg said that he cannot remove the keys from the ignition if the car is left in drive, and then turned off. I'll have to check that out.

MAY 9

Bob and Susan brought Molly over for another play date. Buddy, another littermate, joined us for the first time. We were experiencing very high winds, in the 50-mile-per-hour range, but I saw no reason to cancel the get-together. Garry,

Buddy's owner, and his daughter were headed here from Pennsylvania. Bob and Susan arrived first. We watched as the winds whipped the ash trees to and fro, directly over us. I suggested that we move down to the lower pen, closer to the barn. Trees in that area had been trimmed more recently. No less than one minute after entering the pen, a 3-foot-long, 10-inch diameter branch came crashing down directly behind my guests. If that limb had hit them, there is no telling the outcome, but it wouldn't have been good. We quickly returned to the upper pen. I kept a watchful eye on the trees swaying overhead.

Molly, Buddy and Cooper got along famously—racing through the pen at high speed. Buddy, however, had not yet been neutered and took a liking to Cooper. While Buddy's temperament was wonderful, his mounting Cooper concerned me. Though he wasn't asserting dominance, from what I could tell, I was concerned over the weight being placed on Cooper's hips. It soon passed, so I didn't interfere. They were having so much fun.

While we talked amongst ourselves, Garry's daughter described the day they brought Buddy home. It was much like our experience. Buddy was shy and distant as well. These three littermates developed very differently. Buddy is more confident. Cooper is more shy and sensitive, and has only come around since being neutered. Buddy demonstrates very social behavior, something which Cooper only exhibited after going under the knife. Molly, on the other hand, has a reactive personality, very leery of strangers. When people approach her, she barks, perhaps in fear. With concern for a too-close encounter, it has been difficult for the owners to socialize her. It's really a catch-22, one that I can tell puts strain on the relationship. I feel especially sorry for Susan who adored her previous dog, a gentle husky. When she speaks of him, I see tears well up in her eyes. I'm sure that over time Molly will take her rightful place in Susan's heart.

MAY 16

Today was Cooper's final training session with Steve. John grudgingly participated. Amy was at work. I was telling Steve how well Cooper was doing. Perhaps as a test, Steve asked if Cooper would "Go to bed," from where we stood in the

basement. I gave it my best, and assertively said, "Cooper, go to bed!" That meant he would have to go upstairs, directly to his crate. The command fell on deaf ears; Cooper just looked at me.

In an early session, Steve suggested that I cut back on Cooper's food, so he's more motivated to comply. "Keep him hungry," he said. The other lesson… "Say it once!"

If Cooper doesn't comply, correct him with "No!" and a quick snap of the leash. Do not repeat yourself—ask just once. Most importantly, be consistent. Everyone in the house needs to speak the same language, when it comes to dog training.

We took a final photo of Steve and Cooper on the front lawn, which Steve wants for his website. Was home training worth $410? I would have to say yes. But *I* may have benefited more than Cooper. Being instructed on how to handle this type of dog, understand the temperament, and take a leadership role was invaluable. In short, the training gave *me* more confidence in handling Cooper. Having Cooper neutered was also key.

MAY 17

In preparation for Level II Obedience training, I needed to get more links for Cooper's prong collar. It is no easy task to keep this big dog under control, so a prong is necessary, particularly when Cooper makes a dash for the car. And though these collars look like a medieval torture device, what's a woman to do? Anyway, I took Cooper into the pet store where the salesclerk was kind enough to fit Cooper's collar with the necessary links.

MAY 18

Amy and I took Cooper to his first Level II Obedience class. Last month, John had taken him to Level I, but Cooper already knew the drill and he had mastered a dozen tricks. The decision was made to enroll him directly into Level II. I guess Cooper skipped a grade.

Amy drove separately; I wondered if she remembered taking one of our goldens to this facility, when she was just 10 years old. It had been the dead of winter, and in a driving snow our car ended up in a ditch, only feet from the driveway we couldn't see. A good Samaritan pulled us out. Here, so many years later, we followed the same route, under a light rain. Only this time I was more careful. When we reached our destination, Amy emerged from her car with a grin on her face, as if to say "Where the hell are we?" I opened my back door, and Cooper hopped out, right into the muddy parking lot.

Entering the building, I was on edge. How would Cooper react to all of the activity—people and other dogs? Cheryl greeted us immediately and offered Cooper a treat, which he took. She quietly asked, "How is he doing?" referring to our past discussions about Cooper's nipping incidents. Long story short, his first Level II Obedience class went very well. Sit, stay and down were all in day's work for Cooper. He didn't react to the other dogs or distractions. Of all the dogs in attendance, I would have to say that Cooper was the most composed. Of course, we have five more weeks to go. That could very well change.

LESSONS LEARNED

✔ Be careful when parking your car. I made a mistake that nearly cost Cooper his life, as he was wedged between the garage door and bumper of my car. Accidents can also happen right in the driveway. On a warm spring morning, a family friend didn't see his Collie sleeping behind his car and backed over him.

✔ Supervise every dog playtime and casual meeting closely. Though they may initially appear to get along, a fight can erupt in an instant. We've been lucky so far; all interactions to date have been positive.

✔ It's important that everyone in the household use the same commands. John has a tendency to speak to Cooper in sentences, like "Get away from that." Cooper

Allowing your dog playtime, with littermates and friendly neighborhood dogs, burns off steam. Renowned animal behaviorist, Dr. Nicholas Dodman, author of *The Well-Adjusted Dog*, says, "A tired dog is a good dog." I couldn't agree more.

understands the "Leave it" command, which is simple and to the point, so I try to reinforce the correct terms.

✔ There are differing opinions on choke and prong collars (also called pinch collars). They can cause "physical and structural damage to dog's necks," according to Dr. Dodman. However, at this stage in Cooper's training, the prong collar is the only thing that gives me some degree of control. I've also read that a prong collar stimulates the guiding bite of the alpha dog, which is how a puppy learns to behave. So I'm in the camp that believes these collars serve a purpose, when used correctly. Once Cooper masters the art of loose leash walking, we'll move to a less restrictive harness.

✔ Having Cooper neutered had a noticeable effect on his behavior. The intensity of his barking at visitors diminished. And when I say "Enough!" the barking stops. Though Steve feels there is no need for Cooper to bark, it may be unrealistic to expect a German shepherd to remain silent. As long as I have control over the barking, it's okay that Cooper lets us know when someone is at the door, especially when I'm in my third-floor office.

MONTH 8: THE EARS? GIVE IT UP!

> "Success consists of going
> from failure to failure without
> loss of enthusiasm."
>
> —*Winston Churchill*

MAY 19

We are getting ready to embark on our fourth major home renovation, a new kitchen. We'll also be installing a chair lift to allow my mother to go up and down the stairs. The chair lift salesman was scheduled to come by the house. My hope was that after home training, and the start of Level II Obedience training, Cooper would be on his best behavior when he arrived. When Cooper heard a car door slam, his ears perked up. We headed down the stairs, but I kept Cooper on a short leash, and I led the way. I had him sitting quietly by my side at that door. It was apparent, as the salesman approached, that he was concerned about the dog—who he would later call "Killer." But nothing happened. Cooper sat patiently while he came to the door. I opened the door and handed the gentleman a biscuit. Cooper accepted; a great sign. As the salesman entered the room, I gave Cooper some slack on the leach, so he sniffed and circled around him. Not one bark, nor growl. I'm starting to think that Cooper could one day be a therapy dog, but that might be jumping the gun.

MAY 25

Tonight was Cooper's second Level II Obedience training class. Cooper would see Molly, his favorite playmate. Of course, they came into the world together. Susan, Molly's owner, had just had surgery on her hand, following an injury sustained during a volleyball game. Cheryl called us into class, cutting that conversation short. During the session, I was clumsy, with Cooper often in slow motion compared to the more active and enthusiastic dogs. But overall, we did well. The only distraction was the barking outbursts of two female shepherds in the class. Even though they both knew Cooper, we kept a safe distance.

MAY 28

This closes the book on my effort to set Cooper's ears. Amy said, "Give it up!" She then slit the tape connected the ears, and I removed the pink sponge curler and tape. The left ear immediately flopped, so I wonder if another three weeks would have made any difference. The daily doses of cottage cheese and Knox gelatin certainly didn't. Even scaffolding made of Breathe-Right strips didn't work. After a total of four separate tapings, I would say that the results diminished over time. Perhaps the chemical in the glue undermined the cartilage. This experience makes me wonder if doing nothing to Cooper's ears would have been the better course of action, or inaction, as it were.

JUNE 1

Barb brought Kona over. We were hoping that Kona and Cooper could both join us on our frequent walks. It was not to be. Kona is the more dominant dog. That behavior was on display when she picked up a tiny stick, which Cooper then took an interest in. But as Kona dropped the twig at her feet, Cooper moved in to investigate. Kona was having no part of that, curling her upper lip, exposing a very scary set of teeth. No growling, just a "don't mess with me" attitude that was very effective; Cooper promptly backed off. Maybe one day we'll walk these dogs side by side, but it wouldn't be today.

JUNE 5

I undertook a major project today, repairing the craters that Cooper dug in the yard. But before work could begin, Cooper and I picked up the necessary supplies at Home Depot—top soil, grass seed, metal posts and durable plastic mesh. After I filled the five or so holes, I erected a barrier, isolating both Cooper and Ozzie from the landscaped portion of the yard. They can now do their business on the gravel. And after eight months of havoc wrought upon my garden, I can once again enjoy watching grass grow.

JUNE 6

At long last, I played the video that Cooper's breeder loaned me, *Calming Signals: What does your dog tell you?* The film is narrated by a renowned expert in canine body language,

Turid Rugass, from Norway. Much can be learned from a dog's body language, which can help you "get on talking terms" with your pet. Knowing canine body language can also help you understand how dogs communicate with one another. For instance, to avoid conflict with another dog, your dog will turn his head away or from side to side. It's also best to approach a dog from the side, rather than head-on.

JUNE 12

Amy took Cooper for a run today. I recently read that you should wait until a dog reaches 18 months of age before running long distances. I confirmed this fact with Cooper's vet. Regrettably, I had to tell Amy no more runs with Cooper until next year.

JUNE 13

Cooper's new collar arrived at the pet store. He was bursting out of his old black nylon collar, with psychedelic peace symbols. This collar was more substantial, leather with an engraved plaque. A waste of money really, since no one will see it through his long coat. As we stood at the counter, an overweight Bernese mountain dog sauntered by. This resident dog was not interested in Cooper. It was the toddler running up and down the aisles that caught Cooper's eye, and not in a comforting way. In his mind, I suspect that this child looked like a potential meal. Since Cooper is not familiar with toddlers, I kept a tight grip on his leash. The father then approached us, asking if his child could pet Cooper, I said, "He's in training." That's code for "It's best that he not."

LESSONS LEARNED

✔ On a German shepherd, ears may or may not go up. Obviously, we had mixed results—one up, one down. Despite a tremendous amount of time and effort, including a regimen of Knox Gelatin and cottage cheese, it was for naught. His look has gone from formidable to approachable. If more people are inclined to engage with Cooper, this could work in his favor. Let's say the glass is half full.

✔ Interaction between small children and dogs requires close supervision. Our frequent walks through town and our store visits expose Cooper to some children, but I don't initiate any meet-and-greets. If older kids want to pet Cooper, I give them a treat to offer him. That keeps them from moving in too close. Though I'm confident Cooper would not act badly, it's in everyone's best interest to manage the situation. In time, I'll be able to tell if Cooper is trustworthy.

> If you wish to preserve the beauty of your yard, you'll need a fenced area just for the dog. Letting your dog run loose, tethering him to a tree or putting him on a zip line are not good options. Doing so endangers the public and the dog.

✔ Clips from the video *Calming Signals: What does your dog tell you?* can be seen on YouTube (*www.youtube.com*). Search "Turid Rugass Calming Signals." It's important to understand how dogs communicate through body language. This can be invaluable when handling your dog, particularly in public. I now watch the posture of approaching dogs, as well as Cooper's posture. If things don't look amicable, I keep moving. For instance, if Cooper lowers his head, showing fear, that's not a good signal. Unfortunately, he's not a tail wagging type of dog, so I can't gauge his internal state that way. My clues come more from his head and ear position. If he's uncomfortable, his head lowers slightly, while his pace slows. He's very much on alert. Ears are forward, as if trying to determine if there's a threat. Each encounter is new and different, so over time you pick up on your dog's state of mind.

Month 9:
No Water Dog

"If at first you don't succeed, try, try again.
Then quit. There's no point in being
a damn fool about it."

—*W. C. Fields*

June 19

A routine trip to the bank included Amy and Cooper. I needed to show Amy how to access our safe deposit box—should I get hit by a truck. Cooper trotted into the bank willingly. It was not until we returned to the car that things went awry. Amy heard Cooper begin to wretch, the dreaded sound before a dog vomits. I was oblivious. She said, "Pull over!" I quickly navigated the car into the car wash parking lot, just as he let loose with a torrent of something unimaginable— cat litter and poo! He must have been exploring the cat's litter pan earlier in the day. I had no idea he had helped himself. As I opened the passenger door, I said, "Cooper, stay!" so he didn't traipse through the mess sitting on a brand new blanket. Amy yelled, "Throw the whole thing out!" I scooped up the blanket and tossed it into a nearby trash bin. The granular mass was only an inch away from seeping into the back seat, never to be seen again. Needless to say, we opened all the windows and prayed that there would be no encore. I then wondered aloud what would have happened if he had upchucked in the bank. Undoubtedly, a "No Dogs!" sign would have been posted on the front door.

JUNE 23

I've come to the conclusion that the roll-over command is no longer in favor, as Cooper now hesitates. I'm suspecting that this big dog does not feel comfortable swinging his sizable body back and forth, as he did when he was half the size. He is happy to just go in circles, play dead or shake.

JUNE 26

Stuart cracks me up. He likened John's habit of chasing Cooper around the kitchen and living room to Marlon Brando in *The Godfather*, playing hide and seek with his grandson in the vegetable garden, just before succumbing to a massive heart attack. I must say, Cooper loves the keep-away game. With a toy securely in his mouth, he will dodge any attempt to catch him. Clearly, our lessons in fetch have failed miserably.

JUNE 27

Cooper had his first experience with water—a large body of water—Round Valley Reservoir. While he did tiptoe into the lake, he is no water dog. I threw sticks, got in the water myself, yet nothing really worked. Persistence paid off, for just a moment. He came in toward me, stepping into the deeper waters and struggling to stay afloat. He immediately circled back to terra firma. That was it. He wanted nothing more to do with water. That feeling was only solidified by another large dog that was also experiencing water for the first time. Suddenly, the dog went at Cooper. The dog was leashed, so no harm done—just rattled nerves. Cooper could not wait to get back into the truck. But before heading home, we watched the comings and goings of the many kayakers. Two huge Newfoundland dogs were playing in the water as well. I thought if Cooper watched them, their enthusiasm for water would rub off. And just as we were ready to leave, a female German shepherd puppy and her owners passed by, heading toward the dock. Cooper was interested in following, so he led the way. I wondered how he would handle the dock, projecting into the water some 30 feet. He hesitated as we stepped on the shaky aluminum surface. I was patient, knowing that the puppy, only 20 feet away, might change Cooper's mind. It did. We made our way down the dock, and chatted with the folks. As Cooper began to fidget, I realized his paws were burning on the hot metal dock. He's too heavy to pick up, so I wished the folks well with their new pup and we headed home.

JULY 3

Having told John how well Cooper was doing with the newspaper trick, he tried it out himself. This concerned me. Would Cooper listen to John while off leash? I just had to report the outcome to Cheryl. Thankfully, it was good news.

To: Cheryl
From: D. Phillips

I just had to share this proud moment. Cooper has been taught to get the newspaper, where he's allowed outside the gate, off leash, to grab the paper sitting on the driveway. He also enjoys hunting for it, if it's tossed in the shrubs or gutter. I check to see if anyone is walking, jogging or biking—out of caution. My husband isn't as concerned. He opened the gate, and he and Cooper were looking straight at a passing jogger, with her dog in tow. Cooper was fixed on them, but did not make any move. John simply said, "No!" and Cooper turned around and followed him back through the gate. So he was under control, and not just with me. Another round of Level II Obedience will help reinforce his good behavior.

So after a rocky start, Cooper has turned into the nicest dog ever. And I did take him to Round Valley, but while he was testing the water and paddling around, a dog lunged at him. That really threw him off, but he'll be romping there with Molly and Lucy soon. That should loosen him up. Thanks for your help with Cooper and we'll see you in July.

JULY 4

Fourth of July! How would Cooper handle fireworks? We have learned that he takes thunder and lightning in stride, but how about the ear-piercing bangs and booms all around the area. We are in a rural community, but backyard firework enthusiasts abound. Aren't fireworks in Jersey illegal? Much to our surprise, Cooper was fine. Ozzie, on the other hand, hid behind the cat litter pan and wasn't found until the next day.

JULY 7

Cooper is fixated on squirrels. As they scamper along the top of the fence line of his pen, the critters are not aware that Cooper is lurking nearby. With lightning-fast speed, he shoots straight for them. If not for a last-second leap to higher ground, today's little fellow would have bit the dust.

JULY 10

Since Cooper was not fond of water, we thought we would give it another try. Sounds crazy, but we made a play date with Molly's owners. Kathy, with her dog Lucy, joined us. What a sight, three German shepherds in the water. While the two female shepherds seemed to enjoy the water on this

muggy day, Cooper moved very gingerly. I thought that the other dogs might inspire him to take the plunge. It was not to be. Still, Cooper is no water dog.

JULY 11

John and I took Cooper to watch Amy participate in her third Sprintin Clinton event, a 5K run. Even with the crowds and loud DJ, Cooper kept his composure. But we noticed that people are no longer drawn to him as they were when he was a puppy. John laments the loss of his "chick magnet."

JULY 15

Chasing Meeko, the cat, is still a favorite pastime for Cooper. I tried to stop this behavior, using a soda can filled with coins. Every time Cooper dashes after the cat, I'd slam the can to the floor. This irritated John and Amy to no end, since they get no warning. So this caught everyone's attention, including Cooper's—although only momentarily. Since the cat seems to enjoy the attention, somewhat, I've begun to look the other way. If the cat is seriously objecting to his hind legs being chewed on, I'll intervene with "Easy," which tells Cooper to back off. I reward this behavior when he stops what he is doing and trots over to me—obviously looking for a treat.

LESSONS LEARNED

✔ Training tip (from multiple sources): fill an empty soda can with some pennies and seal the top with duct tape. Whenever the dog is doing something he shouldn't, like chasing the cat, slam the can to the floor. I've employed this technique on occasion. One problem: if anyone else is in the room, you risk reprimand. I'll also admit that this has had limited impact on Cooper's drive to torment the cat.

✔ If the dog is riding in your car, invest in a fitted seat cover just for that purpose. After our close call with vomit, we purchased the perfect hammock-style seat cover from *www.drsfosterandsmith.com.*

✔ Handing treats to a large puppy, with sharp teeth, has its challenges. Cooper's natural tendency is to snap it out of my fingers. I use the word "Gentle" to instruct Cooper to go easy. If I forget to use the command, he clamps down on my fingers.

> When strangers hand Cooper a treat, I've found it best to have them place it in the palm of their hand, as if feeding a horse. That forces the dog to tilt his head and slowly retrieve the treat.

If that happens, I don't let go of the treat. I repeat the process, saying "Gentle," and he slowly takes the treat.

✔ A German shepherd may not take to water. Even in the heat of the summer, Cooper was unwilling to venture in beyond his elbows. I thought all dogs liked water. I was wrong.

✔ As one trainer suggested, be the most interesting thing in the world to your puppy. That means keeping treats in your pocket. This does gives me more control over Cooper. If he isn't listening—specifically when outdoors, I say, "Want a biscuit?" He's front and center in a flash. I lavish him with praise and he gets a treat.

✔ If you have one or more cats, keep the litter away from your puppy, particularly the clumping type. If he consumes enough, it can cause constipation and possible gastrointestinal obstruction. All of our dogs have shown a fondness for cat feces, which some dog people call "Tootsie Rolls."

✔ Dogs and cats can be friends, but it's always better to introduce a puppy to a cat, not the other way around. Meeko has seniority, so Cooper respects the cat. But since Meeko can grow impatient with Cooper's relentless attention, I clip Meeko's razor-sharp nails once a week— without fail. Better that than Meeko tearing through Cooper's lip or nose. Since Cooper's reflexes are excellent, I don't worry too much about Meeko taking an eye out.

Month 10:
Cooper Turns One

"Do not make the mistake of treating your dogs like humans or they will treat you like dogs."

—Martha Scott

JULY 28

CNN posted a January 2010 press release from the American Kennel Club (AKC) about the top 10 dogs in registration numbers. I was surprised to learn that the German Shepherd Dog had overtaken the Yorkshire terrier for the #2 spot, behind Labrador retrievers. As a new German shepherd owner, with no knowledge of where the breed ranked, I wondered why they were so popular.

The AKC attributes the uptick in German shepherd popularity to the nation's on-going military and security efforts home and abroad. We watch these working dogs on the nightly news, searching for survivors of natural and manmade disasters or scouring airports for bombs or drugs. Could viewing a newscast be sending subliminal messages that make us choose a German shepherd? Are we seeking to gain a semblance of control in an uncertain world? I know we feel more secure having Cooper in the house. Even if Steve is right and "Cooper won't take a bullet for us," it is nonetheless a comfort to know that anyone approaching the house—with ill intent—will beat a hasty retreat when hearing a German shepherd bark. Indeed, dogs have been referred to as the world's oldest security system.

AUGUST 16

It's Cooper's birthday! He's one year old. I'm not sure if I've ever remembered one of our dogs' birthdays. Without a doubt, Cooper is an important part of our family. Amazingly intelligent, playful, and always eager to please, Cooper has a permanent place in our hearts. Despite our affection for this dog, I did not go so far as to bake a biscuit cake or anything. We did, however, pause during dinner to acknowledge the one-year milestone and marvel at how much progress Cooper has made. The frightened puppy, which Stu called "Big Scary Dog," is now a more confident dog who is comfortable with his place in the Phillips pack.

AUGUST 17

Cooper completed his second Level II Obedience training this evening. Before leaving, I asked Cheryl if she thought Cooper could become a therapy dog. At one year of age, he is comfortable around my mother's wheelchair, walker and canes. Why not? Her response was, "No. He doesn't like people."

Nothing more was said. It was a disappointing but understandable assessment. Perhaps nature has prevailed over nurture, but we'll still keep at it— socializing that is.

AUGUST 20

John and I decided to take an unplanned trip to North Carolina; the timing just seemed right. What about Cooper and Ozzie? When I talked about putting them in a kennel, Amy said, in no uncertain terms, "I want Cooper here with me." That was a pleasant surprise. She feels more comfortable with Cooper in the house.

LESSONS LEARNED

✔ With consistent training, a once-shy puppy can grow into a more confident adult dog. At one year, Cooper has made remarkable strides. But I've been told by his trainer that the socialization of a German shepherd can take up to three years. So the game plan is to continue taking Cooper everywhere and anywhere, whether he likes it or not.

✔ Not only are German shepherds the second most popular dog in the United States, they are ranked #3 in intelligence, behind the border collie and standard poodle, which rank #1 and #2, respectively. For more about *The Top 10 Smartest Dog Breeds in the World*, visit *www. petmedsonline.org/top-10-smartest-dogs-in-the-world.html.*

✔ Despite your best efforts to socialize a dog, he may not be therapy dog material. Cooper is far more social, but he's not delighted to see someone walk through the door, unless it's John, Amy or me.

✔ Though I like to think a dog is a more effective theft deterrent than an security system, I'm wrong. While a German shepherd is a reliable sentry, experts feel a burglar alarm is better protection. Besides being safer and less expensive, you don't have to feed an alarm system or take it to the vet. More importantly, it can't bite someone. However, an alarm system can't give a homeowner unconditional love.

Month 11:
The Ultimate Test

> "I think that a dog tries much harder to understand us than we do him."
>
> —*Wilma Melville*

AUGUST 21

Over the past year, I've been subconsciously making comparisons between our many golden retrievers and Cooper.

- Cooper does not retrieve thrown toys and sticks. He'll come close to me with a toy, but then quickly turn away. His reflexes are astonishing. When ignored, he'll drop the toy in my lap. The goldens wanted nothing more than to give you the toy. How else would they be able to retrieve?

- When at rest, Cooper doesn't dream, with legs thrashing about and making whining noises, as did the goldens, who appeared to be hunting water fowl. Cooper rests with his eyes partially open, perhaps an adaptation necessary to protect a flock of sheep; this dog is ready to respond to any danger—like an approaching coyote, fox or burglar.

- Cooper does not bark incessantly, either inside the house or while in the pen. Unlike the goldens that barked nonstop, Cooper is quiet, unless a foolish squirrel or passing whitetail deer catches his eye.

- Cooper is digging a hole to China, but in the middle of the pen. The goldens only dug along the perimeter, in order to escape. Failing that, they learned to scale the fence. Cooper is no climber.

- Our male goldens had the dreadful habit of eating their own stools, a behavior called coprophagy. Cooper shows no such interest. On the contrary, he instinctively does his business as far away from the house as possible. And, without any special training, he has a specific spot. Our job is to keep that spot clean.

- The goldens also had serious flatulence, a noxious gas that must have been the byproduct of eating their own stools. Those dogs could clear a room—of people—in an instant. I have yet to "get wind" of Cooper.

AUGUST 28

I took Cooper for a walk through town—in 90-plus degree heat. I planted myself on a shaded bench, with Cooper lying by my side. Many passersby admired my handsome pooch, but one family of four stopped directly in front of Cooper. One young lady asked, "Can we pet your dog?" I said, "Sure. Just extend your hand." As I demonstrated, Cooper's low growl caught me by surprise. He had not growled at anyone in public since he was four months old. While I said, "No!" to Cooper, in retrospect, it was not forceful enough. I handed her a bacon treat to give to him. Cooper started to stand up, sniffing the treat, she backed up, and then dropped it on the ground. That unpleasant meet-and-greet made me pause to consider the possibility that Cooper could lunge at someone.

SEPTEMBER 2

Cooper succeeded in sneaking his volleyball into the house. This tripping hazard is best left outside, but he loves that tattered sphere. I've tried switching

to tennis balls—so much easier to throw—but it's to no avail.

SEPTEMBER 6

Labor Day parade! Every year we attend the largest parade in New Jersey, held in South Plainfield—John's hometown. This year, we made the pilgrimage with Cooper. We met up with Dad, who still lives in town, as well as Rich and Brian. Brian hadn't seen Cooper since the dog was just three months old; he took an immediate liking to Cooper. Once settled into our curbside seats, Cooper was his constant companion, as was

another unwelcome young fellow.

A family standing nearby with a rambunctious little boy, about 5 years old, was paying no attention to his antics. That

child was intent on getting to Cooper. While I wished I could have welcomed him up to Cooper for a visit, there was just too much commotion—fire engine sirens blaring, car horns honking, which made me feel it best to keep Cooper at my side. That didn't prevent the boy from dashing to and fro in front of Cooper, who kept a close eye on the little guy. Cooper didn't appear stressed, but I wasn't going to let down my guard. If the boy decided to rush in, Cooper might not take kindly to the intrusion—but, again, I wasn't sure.

Cooper has had virtually no exposure to babies and toddlers. And thinking back to what Cheryl said in Level II Obedience, "Running children can be viewed as prey by a dog." That knowledge made me extra-vigilant. But lo and behold, while we stood to watch antique cars pass by, suddenly the boy dashed over and poked Cooper in the hindquarters. I saw nothing, just the boy running away and turning back with a devilish grin on his face; he had achieved his goal of touching the big dog. I didn't know what had happened until Rich caught my eye and motioned in that direction. I then turned to look at Cooper; he was unfazed, which was what anyone would hope for. Cooper tolerated relentless teasing.

After 45 minutes of trying, the boy succeeded in confronting

a dog three times his size. And while some might think I'm foolish for not allowing this child to approach initially, and satisfy his curiosity, I actually had allowed a quieter, even younger boy, to pet Cooper. His parents were right beside him and they asked, "Can our son pet your dog?" I said, "Sure. Just reach out your hand so he can sniff." Cooper was lying on the ground, so the little tyke knelt and extended his tiny hand. He then slowly reached in to pet Cooper on the head. Only the second time Cooper was faced with a little child, I'll admit I was nervous, but saw no warning signs that he might object.

Unsupervised children are the more frequent victims of the one million dog bites that occur each year. While I never would have brought Cooper to a public place if I suspected he was dangerous in any way, I never expected parents to allow their small child to harass a big dog. They paid no attention whatsoever to what their child was doing. In retrospect, I should have pulled them aside. Thankfully, the event ended without incident.

SEPTEMBER 8

The cat, Meeko, has recently been given outdoor privileges, ever since he decided to use the rec room rug as a toilet. He is happier and enjoying his newfound freedom, chasing chipmunks and depositing dead mice at the back door. And with Cooper being the instigator of cat-dog confrontations, I'm now enjoying some peace and quiet. Only one unfortunate fact: rarely have our outdoors cats survived for very long. Imagine the Steven King movie, *Pet Cemetery*, only with passenger cars, not 18-wheelers, speeding by the house. Our beloved Tori, a massive Maine Coon cat, and affectionate Abyssinian, Woody, both left this earth too soon. Nevertheless, Meeko has been banished from the house during the day. He is quite content to come in at night, and there hasn't been an accident (inside the house) since.

SEPTEMBER 10

Cooper has not shown any aggressive greeting behavior when a visitor stops by since he was formally trained by Steve. However, my mother's power chair repairman did get startled when Cooper met him at the door. In fact, the guy high-tailed it, literally, back to his van; perhaps he had seen the *Beware of Dog* sign. But as I opened the door, the gentleman turned back to see that I had Cooper under control. As he came back to the door, I simply had him give Cooper a biscuit and all was well. What was more alarming to Cooper was the power chair itself. Now that my 89-year-old mother had moved into the main house, there was a strange new mechanical device silently navigating the rooms, with my mother at the controls. When she entered the kitchen today, without announcing herself, Cooper was good for three strong barks, but quickly calmed down. I asked Cheryl how to address this behavior. She suggested attaching a bell to the chair. I did just that by duct-taping a small bell to the wheel. Problem solved. After only a few days, the bell fell off. By then, Cooper was fully adjusted to our new pack member.

SEPTEMBER 14

One of John's customers, the one who gave him the book *The Art of Raising a Puppy*, had sad news. His beloved German shepherd, Heidi, had died of cancer. She was only four years old. When Cooper was only a puppy, this gentleman told John, "Once you own a German shepherd, no other breed will do."

SEPTEMBER 16

Meeko needed his rabies vaccination, so I secured him in his carrier and asked Cooper, "Want to go for a ride?" That always gets him excited, as he rushed over to the basket looking for his leash. I wanted to get a reading on his weight while we were there. As we waited our turn, Cooper just chilled. Other dogs were shaking and pacing. Not Cooper. Unlike our past big dogs, there is no fussing and trying to climb into my lap. Cooper just seems to shut down in high-stress settings.

When we entered the exam room, Meeko got his vaccination and Cooper's weight was 77 pounds. The vet tech felt his rib cage and thought he was somewhat underweight. Dr. Reynolds agreed. So the plan is to feed Cooper twice a day. He has been eating just one meal for many months. Breakfast was never of much interest. I would have to entice him with more appealing choices.

I also mentioned that Cooper was scooting his butt across the carpet. Picture the television commercial where the woman yells "Toby, No!" That's me. Dr. Reynolds said that behavior mostly likely meant impacted anal glands. Very unpleasant indeed. He was going to do some probing and pulled on latex surgical gloves. The vet tech held Cooper around the chest as Dr. Reynolds went in. He could not extract any fluid from one side; apparently there are two glands. The other gland was hard to the touch. He suggested antibiotics, to reduce any infection that might be present. While I thought Cooper could have worms, that was not the cause. He wants to see us back in a week.

SEPTEMBER 18

I learned that my Uncle Tom once owned a shepherd by the name of Gretchen. A gift to Wade and Sarah Bryan, my cousins, I could tell that they were very fond of that dog. In the 1960s, Gretchen stood guard over their home in Chicago. The neighborhood was the target of multiple break-ins, yet they had no such trouble. While an excellent guard dog, Gretchen was also a favorite playmate of the neighborhood kids. Uncle Tom would hear the doorbell ring and, more often than not, it was the kids asking, "Can Gretchen come out to play?" Before he could even respond, Gretchen would scamper out the door.

One day, a little boy asked Uncle Tom if he was interested in selling Gretchen. Upon hearing, "Sorry, she's not for sale," the boy said, "Can I trade one of my three sisters for the dog?" Uncle Tom responded with, "Well, you'd better first check with your mother." The boy wasn't seen again for three weeks, possibly grounded by a mother who was not amused.

LESSONS LEARNED

✔ Taking a dog out in 90-degree heat may make him irritable. I can't be sure it was the heat, but Cooper has only growled in public twice, once at Amy's workplace and once in town. Though the growl was quick—no lip curling, no barking—it means the dog was outside his comfort zone. That just tells me we need to get into town more often. Repetition is the only answer. He'll learn that there is nothing to fear.

✔ Include the dog in all outdoor activities, even parades. Cooper went to his first parade on Labor Day, getting a sizable dose of people, kids, clowns, dogs, cars, trucks, fire engines, you name it.

> When in public, keep an eye out for unsupervised children. They are drawn to dogs like bears to bird feeders.

✔ If a dog is protective by nature, placing a *Beware of Dog* sign in the window can forewarn delivery and service people. Though we are not *Beware of Dog*-sign people, we posted one outside the back door.

✔ The American Veterinary Medical Association *Task Force on Canine Aggression and Human-Canine Interactions* reports that dog bite injuries rank third only to bicycle and baseball/softball injuries as a leading cause of emergency admission of children to hospitals.

Putting children at risk are their natural behaviors, including running, yelling, grabbing, hitting, quick and darting movements, and maintaining eye contact.

✔ Feeding a dog twice a day is often recommended, even after one year of age. Cooper, however, shows no interest in a morning meal. Helping him to gain a few pounds won't be easy. It's just as well, since shepherds are better kept on the lean side; less weight on hips that may one day suffer from dysplasia.

MONTH 12:
DOG PARK REVISITED

**"The greatness of a nation and its moral progress
can be judged by the way its animals are treated."**

—Mahatma Gandhi

SEPTEMBER 19

We took a chance, leaving Amy in charge of animal care for the first time. I had wanted to leave the dogs at a kennel, but Amy insisted that she could handle the responsibility. One problem: she was in Boston. Nonetheless, we went with the flow, packing up and leaving for our annual family golf outing, what we fondly call the Phillips Hackfest. If anything were to go wrong, we were only an hour from home. The dogs were secured in the kitchen, the cat in the bathroom—near the litter, and away we went. Amy was expected home by dinner time, just in time to let the dogs out. Wouldn't you know, my cell phone rang while we were eating dinner. It was nearly 10:00 p.m., way past her arrival time. She had gotten lost on a return trip from Massachusetts, taking the wrong exit after crossing the George Washington Bridge. I don't know if I was annoyed, terrified or both. Where was she? How long had the dogs been locked in the kitchen? I handed the phone to John, since he could give her better directions. Two hours later, she arrived home safely. And to my surprise, the dogs had held their bladders for over 12 hours. Close call—on all counts.

SEPTEMBER 24

I had to make a trip to the paint store, so Cooper was in tow. That is one place where Cooper is sure to get some attention. He usually just lies down and watches all of the activity. Eric, the sales manager, tells John that when he sees Cooper he's not sure whether to run or give him a biscuit. I prefer the latter. People often have stories about growing up with a German shepherd, typically fond memories. Today was no different, as one gentleman told me all about his son rescuing a shepherd in the aftermath of Hurricane Katrina.

SEPTEMBER 25

After two years of promising Greg that John and I would paint his porch in Brooklyn, it's finally happening. This is payback for his drafting plans for our kitchen addition. Amy wasn't around to dog-sit, so Cooper came with us. What an operation, placing Cooper's huge crate in John's van. Other than a few whining episodes, Cooper tolerated the 1-1/2-hour trip well. The real chore was separating Cooper and Loki, my niece Emily's dog. He's not very fond of Cooper. I can't blame him. Loki is a six-year-old border collie that is simply protecting his home turf. Unfortunately, this meant Cooper had to spend a considerable amount of time in his crate. When I felt sorry for him and released him from his cell, he promptly got into the paint. Ugh! Back he went. Later that evening before heading home, Cooper was taken on one last outing to the backyard. As we approached the door, my sister-in-law Julie said, "Watch out for the raccoons." Just a few hours earlier, during our walk through Prospect Park, we encountered a rat. Raccoons and rats? We don't see this much scary wildlife in our neck of the woods, and we live in the woods.

SEPTEMBER 27

Cooper has made great strides in socializing with other dogs at doggy daycare. Stephanie is Cooper's favorite caregiver and Sophie is his favorite playmate. Today, I had a chance to talk with Linda, the owner. I asked if she thought Cooper could

become a therapy dog, even though his trainer had said, "No. He does not like people." Linda has a therapy dog that doesn't necessarily "like" people. The dog simply follows her

command to jump on a patient's lap. Her assessment of Cooper at this stage makes me hopeful that he could bring a smile to patients' faces one day.

OCTOBER 2

Greg and Stuart were recruited to help move my mother's furniture from her apartment to the main house. These visits always give me an opportunity to test Cooper. Both guys were able to enter the house without stirring Cooper's ire. They simply said, "Hi Cooper," which disarms him. Having a biscuit bowl sitting on the rec room pool table doesn't hurt either.

I think over the past six month, the guys have taken a liking to Cooper, calling him "Big Dog," and tossing him treats or toys. Stuart is still under a three-year contract with a Maryland energy firm, and misses his chocolate Labrador back home in Arizona. Cooper is the next best thing. Those two have really bonded since their not-so-pleasant first encounter, a.k.a., ass nipping.

OCTOBER 4

Barb made Cooper a bandana, just the right size. I slipped it over his collar, and he was transformed into a fashionable canine. Barb said the fabric is similar to something that Harley Davidson riders use; I'm guessing for those bandanas they wrap around their heads. Is that a du-rag? Whatever it is, we like its fire and flame theme, as Halloween is approaching.

OCTOBER 8

It is rutting season, the time of year when the whitetail deer are looking for mates. Deer are everywhere—destroying all of our shrubbery, save for the odorous boxwood. My fear is that Cooper will dash off in pursuit of these hooved rats, as we fondly call them. Brazen and unafraid, the deer come right up to the house. Today, I caught a buck and doe pausing in front of the barn. The doe ran off as the buck was momentarily confronting a rival—his own reflection in the barn window. Camera in hand, I thought we might be witness to his charging headlong into the glass, but was relieved as he raced up the driveway, as if suddenly remembering that it was breeding season.

OCTOBER 9

Cooper joined John and me on a trip to pick up a motorized recliner for Mom. It must be quite a sight to see Cooper sitting between us in the pick-up truck. This dog's head towers over John. Of course, we should have Cooper secured somehow. He was much safer in the back of my SUV. There, too, he should be tethered. An unrestrained dog is a deadly projectile in an accident. When we travel to Greg's house, Cooper goes in the cargo compartment or in a crate. Molly's owners really have the safest method, a halter that goes around the dog's chest and body, which is then attached to a leash that is attached to a cord that extends from one side of the passenger compartment to the other. Molly is free to roam, but is secure in case of a sudden stop. I need to investigate this type of rigging.

OCTOBER 10

Sunday morning, and John and I were enjoying the newspaper. Immersed in our reading, Meeko was crying to be let outside. Both of us ignored the irritation, waiting for the other person to get up and open the door. Even Cooper chose to remain at my feet. When the cat's cries became too loud to ignore, John got up to open the door. As Meeko dashed out, Cooper, without budging and with perfect timing, groaned, as if to say, "Thank you!" Even he was annoyed by that cat.

OCTOBER 13

Cooper was referred to by one family friend as "the most educated dog in Hunterdon County," which makes me chuckle. But we have been told that German shepherds need a lot of training. So I'm guessing that we're two years away from a well-adjusted, trustworthy companion. And with that knowledge, we forge ahead, enrolling him in another class; K9 Nose Work seemed like the best fit. In this workshop, dogs are taught to find a treat with their nose, of course.

Our first Nose Work class went off without a hitch. Cooper's not terribly food-motivated, so I held off on giving him dinner. That made him slightly more driven to find smelly, meat treats—kielbasa. When it was Cooper's turn, I said, "Find it!" He understands that means there was something on the other side of the wall, something tasty. Sniffing from box to box, he's finally rewarded. This exercise was repeated with increasing difficulty. Boxes are placed in more out-of-the-way places and at higher levels. This class was purely for fun, no obedience involved. However, dogs can be certified in this discipline. I doubt we will take it that far.

P.S. I learned tonight that nuts are not good for dogs. Nearly every night, John tosses peanuts to Cooper, who loves snapping them out of the air. Nancy, a friend from class, told me that macadamia nuts are particularly toxic to dogs.

OCTOBER 16

For only the second time, Amy took Cooper on an outing to her friend's house. Cooper and their family dog, Joey, play well together, so I was thrilled that Cooper had a chance to get out for the day. They took the dogs to a dog park in Echo Lake Park, where my childhood friends and I used to bike and boat. Amy said the dogs had a great time. Having not had much success in my two prior trips to a dog park, I was delighted that all went well. This dog park, unlike our local park, segregates dogs based on their size—small, medium and large. This type of arrangement in Flemington would have prevented Cooper's unfortunate encounter with five little dogs that wanted to play, but could only demonstrate their affection for him by nipping at his hindquarters.

LESSONS LEARNED

✔ Doggy daycare has been far more valuable that I initially thought. As long as the dog is not aggressive with other dogs, there's no reason he shouldn't have playtime outside the home. I attribute much of Cooper's positive development to just a few hours a week at a happy place.

✔ When riding in the car, the puppy should be secured in a crate (in the cargo compartment) or tethered in the back seat. In the event of an accident, a loose dog can be injured or become a dangerous projectile. For an excellent overview of car safety systems for your dog, refer to *Happy Tails Across New Jersey, Things to See and Do with Your Dog in the Garden State*, by Diane Goodspeed. The author, who travels extensively with her dogs, details the pros and cons of dog carriers, harnesses, and even booster seats for smaller dogs.

✔ Also when riding in the car, don't let the dog hang his head out the window. Though Cooper has no interest in letting his jowls flap in the wind, many dogs do. In fact, I allowed all of our goldens to do so. I've only recently been informed that a rock (or other debris) kicked up from a tire can cause serious injury or death. Case in point was an adopted greyhound that lost an eye. And while we're on the subject, never let a dog ride in the bed of a pick-up truck. That's just plain crazy.

- German shepherds excel at K9 Nose Work. That's why they are the ideal police dog, searching out bad guys, drugs and bombs. And though Cooper will never be put into service, he demonstrated some skill at tracking for treats.

- Certain foods are very dangerous for dogs. For example, a food that is harmless to humans, avocado, should never be given to a dog, not even a chip with guacamole. Avocados contain a chemical called Persin in the leaves, skin, bark, and the fruit itself, which is very bad for dogs. And, did you know that onions and garlic can destroy a dog's red blood cells, leading to anemia? Grapes and raisins are also off limits. The high phosphorus content in nuts, like macadamia, can possibly lead to bladder stones. The list goes on and on. For more information, check out *http:// pets.webmd.com/dogs* and *www.petpoisonhelpline.com/ poisons/*.

- Because of the aforementioned dangerous foods, a puppy needs to know the "Leave it" command. I use that command primarily in the kitchen when forbidden foods falls to the floor, like grapes. On the flip side, I say

Celebrity dog trainer, Victoria Stilwell, author of *It's Me or the Dog: How to Have the Perfect Pet*, says, "96% of dogs that end up abandoned in shelters have never had any training." That's an astonishing statistic. Whether due to lack of time, lack of money and/or indifference, an untrained dog *will* wreak havoc. The consequence: millions of abandoned dogs every year, 50% of which will be destroyed (*www. aspca.org/about-us/faq/pet- statistics.aspx*).

"Crumb" when the morsel is fair game. Cooper can be out of sight, but if I say "Crumb," he's sniffing around my feet within seconds; it's a prompt and effective way to clean the floor.

✔ There are dog parks that separate play areas based on dog size. That's the only type of dog park I would visit, as little dogs may be threatened by larger dogs, increasing the likelihood that the dog (or you) could get bitten.

✔ Tying a bandana around a dog's neck makes the animal more approachable on the street. I've experienced this first-hand with Cooper. Andrea Arden, says, "Because of preconceived notions, some breeds, types or sizes of dog rarely get to meet friendly, calm people outside the family. Try an accessory that will accentuate your dog's friendly nature, such as a brightly colored bandana or teach him to do a couple of cute tricks to encourage social encounters."

MONTH 13: CANINE GOOD CITIZEN—WHY NOT?

"If you're not the lead dog, the view never changes."

—Author Unknown

OCTOBER 20

Our second K9 Nose Work class was much like the first, only now the dogs must find the treat and then sit. This was more challenging since Cooper's first instinct was to consume any morsel under the box or traffic cone. Everyone gets a chance to participate and watching the other dogs work was almost as much fun as taking part. One male pug, named Allen, was hilarious. He was isolated from the group because of his aggression toward other dogs. If he gets even the slightest glimpse of another dog, he goes into a rage. Remarkably, none of the other dogs react. I can only image what's going through their heads as they watch his display of bravado.

OCTOBER 22

A hazard of having a big dog and little dog under one roof—the little dog has doubled in size. Ozzie has gained a lot of weight, feasting on Cooper's leftovers. I have to be more diligent about picking up Cooper's bowl. If not, Ozzie licks it clean.

OCTOBER 24

A trip to Home Depot was a real social event. Nearly every person that crossed Cooper's path stopped to chat. Cooper was now at the point where *he* approaches people, rather than backing away. It may be that he anticipates a treat. So he gently sniffs pant legs and the occasional crotch, which I hesitate to correct for fear of discouraging interaction with people. Thankfully, people don't seem to mind. Most know better than to immediately pat him on the head, instead offering a hand as a way to get acquainted. I'm also better at preventing overly rambunctious people or kids from moving too fast, asking them to just extend a hand.

On our way home, as we passed a playground and ballpark, I noticed a large gathering of people in the parking lot, along with an equal number of German shepherds. They appeared to be disbanding, so I yelled, "Stop the car!" John pulls the truck into the lot, and I hopped out. I said hello to two women sitting on a tailgate and asked if it was an open group. They pointed to another woman and said, "Speak to her." I walked over and introduced myself, explaining that I had a German shepherd and was curious about the group. She asked to meet Cooper. I rushed back to the truck; Cooper bounded out the door, eager to meet both people and dogs, which was encouraging. Two strange dogs and their owners came up and checked Cooper out, including a striking long-coat shepherd. There was not a single sign of stress or aggression toward anyone—human or canine. One gentleman even grabbed Cooper's sides and ran his hands down his body, from shoulders to hips. If that didn't unnerve him, I figured it was a successful "interview." I learned that the group meets every Sunday, rain or shine, to reinforce basic obedience and socialize the dogs. It's just what Cooper needs.

OCTOBER 25

Cooper has enjoyed more freedom around the house and property. And though his greeting behavior was far better, he still needs supervision. On two recent occasions when Barb arrived for our walk, Cooper gently planted his teeth on her posterior, and another time on her arm. In neither case did he bite. It could even be viewed as him happy to see her, since Cooper always joins us on our walks. Could this just be herding behavior?

In the first instance, when Cooper greeted Barb in the driveway, there was no correction. By the time she reached the back porch, the event was long over. On the second occasion, she had entered the rec room on the ground level. Cooper bounded down the basement steps. Before I got there, he mouthed her arm, again teeth to flesh. I quickly reprimanded him, with a stern "No! Bad dog," which gets his attention. And though we always take Cooper on our walks, this time he stayed home as punishment. I'm suspecting that this very smart canine has the intelligence of at least a three-year-old, and he just might think about his actions; at least for a nanosecond. Since those encounters, I have Cooper in a sit-stay in the kitchen, while I go to the rec room and talk to Barb. Cooper does not descend the stairs until told to come. Barb, who is not particularly fond of dogs, was ready with a biscuit, which Cooper accepted. I'm hoping that we have nipped (pun intended) this behavior in the bud.

OCTOBER 27

The third K9 Nose Work class was another fun night out for Cooper. He consistently found his reward. We will have to continue this training between sessions, which I have yet to do. I have, however, gathered a bunch of boxes. I need to mark one "Food" and always place the treat in that box. My plan: scatter boxes around the kitchen and let Cooper find his reward. Working at home will allow me to test him off-leash, which they say lets the dog search with less inhibition. In class, Cooper was always on-leash. At some point, Cooper will be ready to seek out his treats outdoors. That will be the ultimate test to determine whether he was enjoying this new exercise. It is frequently said that German shepherds need a job, so we will continue engaging him in these types of activities.

OCTOBER 31

Today was Cooper's first training session in the park. Fifteen minutes before class, a sizable gathering of German shepherds and their owners had already arrived. There was a puppy training session going on, which made me—momentarily— ponder adding a third dog to the household, but only momentarily. I talked with two gentlemen, both with long-coat shepherds. We talked about ages, origins and behaviors unique to shepherds, including how they mouth your arm when happy to see you. Both men agreed that's just a trait of shepherds.

As we continued to talk, one dog made a sudden move on Cooper. At close range, this was the scariest encounter to date. She didn't connect with Cooper, as the handler had a tight grip on the leash. She was quickly forced to into a down position. With her mouth held closed, the dog—in this context *bitch* might work better—was verbally reprimanded. My only hope was that Cooper understood that aggressive behavior was unacceptable. Another woman later told me that a dog can become aggressive if on the receiving end of such an attack, which I was aware of. I understand that it's important to keep young puppies and dogs away from danger. So far, we've encountered a number of ill-tempered Labs, one while swimming at Round Valley Reservoir, and another territorial Lab running loose in the street. Coincidentally enough, our appliance repair man said that the only dog that ever bit him was a Labrador. Oh, and there was another story from the cable guy. His Labrador bit a neighbor—who it turns out was a police officer. The dog damaged muscles in her rifle arm, impairing her ability to handle a gun. That ended in a lawsuit. But to put the number of incidents with Labradors into perspectives, there are more than twice as many AKC-registered Labradors in the U.S. currently 89,599, versus 40,938 German shepherds*.

* October, 2010. Also see November 13th entry.

As class was about to start, a woman logged everyone's dog on her list and collected $10—a very fair price. There were 15 dogs in attendance. I followed the pack as they formed three lines in the parking lot. The trainer, Bonnie, led the group in exercises back and forth through the parking lot, much like line dancing with dogs. Cooper did well until we encountered new lessons, the one-quarter turn (to the right), sit and back up (to the left), and the sit again. We'll need to practice those moves. We also did a figure eight with three people. I tended to drag Cooper, which was not good. Cooper did know sit, stay, and down though, and appeared unfazed by the commotion of other dogs walking through the park.

Before the final exercise (a recall from across the lot), I talked to a woman who told me her dog passed the Canine Good Citizen (CGC) test. I asked her what the program was about. She explained that it's an AKC certification that tests a dog on a number of things, like meeting strangers, being brushed—10 tests in all. I'll have to research the program more. Maybe I could have Cooper tested.

After class disbanded, Cooper and I strolled up to an elderly couple, one on a scooter and another seated. I said to Cooper, "Say hello." He poked his nose into the gentleman's face, which he seemed to enjoy. They had been admiring Cooper, saying how much larger Cooper was than the other dogs. He's about two inches taller than the breed standard, and very long, but with his large head and very long tail, he's proportional. While we chatted, his wife mentioned how her husband served in Germany during WWII but never saw a single German shepherd. The innuendo: he had more of an eye for the ladies.

Before everyone left, Bonnie said they would be setting up jumps, in case we wanted to do any jumping exercises. Would Cooper jump over a bar set off the ground? I didn't think so, but was once again surprised. A bit awkward, he nonetheless jumped, or tripped, over the bar. We made a few loops. My treats ran out. We called it a day.

This evening, we watched *House on Haunted Hill* with Vincent Price—most appropriate for Halloween. At one point, I looked down to see Cooper dreaming. His back and front legs were twitching. Unlike our past dogs, I have never seen Cooper dreaming, until now. We wondered if he was finally comfortable with his surrounding, and could now enjoy a deep sleep.

NOVEMBER 1

We practiced K9 Nose Work exercises this evening. Cooper was very enthusiastic; the treat was London broil. After scattering boxes around the kitchen, I showed him the "Food" box, with meaty morsels on the bottom. I instructed him to stay in the living room, while I hid the box. Returning to the living room, I said, "Find it!" and he sped past me in search of his treat. Off-leash, he zoomed from box-to-box, quickly locating his reward. The way he jumped into action when he hears the "Find it!" command made me appreciate the intelligence of this breed.

Exactly one year ago, I had expressed concern over Cooper and Meeko becoming buddies. I think that process is complete. No chill pill required. Meeko has learned to move slowly around Cooper, in order to not trigger his prey instinct. As Meeko slinks through the living room, Cooper runs up and mouths his tiny hind legs, almost as if trying to herd the cat.

NOVEMBER 2

Election Day! Mom and I headed to the polls in the afternoon, with Cooper in tow. Mom in a wheelchair and Cooper on a leash; I had my hands full. I just don't like to miss an opportunity for Cooper to socialize. (We occasionally stroll through town, with Cooper trotting alongside her wheelchair. I figured this was good preparation for Cooper becoming a therapy dog, but that day is way off.)

We made it into the polling place, the firehouse, with everyone's eyes on Cooper. There was no one voting, just 10-plus poll workers watching us. Cooper was on his best behavior, allowing people to pet him. One woman asked what breed he was, while another said, "Does he have hip problems?"

I assumed that she considered his conformation of sloping hindquarters a physical defect. I assured her that he was fine.

After casting our votes, we turned for the door; Cooper could have easily pulled Mom's wheelchair without my assistance. He just cannot wait to get back to the car. Is that due to fear of public settings? At this point, he has been everywhere except establishments that serve food or sell fine China, but his unease is still apparent.

P.S. Before we left for the polling place, the *Meals on Wheels* volunteer arrived at the side door. He rapped loudly on the door, which sent Cooper into a barking frenzy. I grabbed Cooper's collar and let the gentleman enter the kitchen. Cooper strained to sniff him, so I gave the man a biscuit. All was fine. Cooper calmed down immediately. This protective behavior at the door was the most pronounced to date. However, he was silenced using the "Enough" command.

NOVEMBER 3

Another chance to test Cooper's greeting behavior. Our heat was on the fritz, just as nighttime temperatures entered the 30s. Bob and Randy, who have been servicing our oil burner for decades, pulled up in their van. When the car doors shut, Cooper's ears perked up. I took a firm grip on Cooper's collar and we headed downstairs. Now no offense to oil serviceman, but that is one smelly profession. How would Cooper react to these guys? As I let them through the door, Cooper was struggling to get close. I just led Cooper around with me, following the men as they began investigating the problem. We retreated to the kitchen, where I rewarded Cooper with a biscuit. But as the men went up and down the stairs, I kept a watchful eye on Cooper's movements. No issues. No cause for concern. In fact, Bob volunteered that the only dog that ever bit him was a Labrador. But as we know, Labs outnumber shepherds 2 to 1; statistically, you would have more encounters.

Cooper had another fun outing at K9 Nose Work this evening. In preparation for class, I did something I've never done before—cooked dog treats. Cooper loved searching for London broil the night before. Why not mix that with greasy pork leftovers? I searched the Internet for a recipe, which gave me a clue as to the ingredients. I blended the meats with egg and corn meal, and baked the concoction—spread out in a thin layer—at 350 degree for 40 minutes. The results, however, were not very odorous. Would Cooper be able to track to the scent? I wasn't disappointed. Cooper quickly found his reward on each of his four tries.

NOVEMBER 4

With Mom now living with us, her twice-weekly *Meals on Wheels* deliveries require that I monitor Cooper. When I work in my office, Cooper is typically outside a gate, at the bottom of the steps. If there were no gate, he would lie outside my door, which once almost sent me tumbling down the stairs. We have since made sure he stays on the first floor. This is only on rainy or snowy days. Otherwise, he's outside in his pen.

If Cooper is inside, I listen for the *Meals* volunteer to arrive and greet him or her at the door, to prevent Cooper from being startled, as he was a few days ago. I asked today's volunteer inside. I handed her a biscuit to give to Cooper, which he took. This woman had a shepherd while growing up. I asked how the dog did with people coming to the house. She responded, "Not good." Without going into further detail, they had to put the dog down due to aggression issues.

NOVEMBER 5

While picking Cooper up from his once-a-week trip to doggy daycare, I asked Linda about Canine Good Citizen certification. She gave me the name of an organization that had just completed testing in our area. Linda has therapy dogs certified by this group, which also does CGC testing. CGC testing is less rigorous than therapy dog testing, so I think we will start with CGC. I'm more confident that Cooper is up to it.

Linda also thought Cooper could pass the CGC test. He has grown from a shy puppy, cowering in the corner, to one that romps with the other dogs. Doggy daycare has been the best thing ever for Cooper. He gets to be with dogs his own size and take commands from other people. Just like everyone should share in dog-feeding duties, so too should dogs be handled by others.

NOVEMBER 6

John and I took Cooper on a mission—to find a permanent solution to the dog gate problem. We can't have Cooper sleeping outside our bedroom door. Our present solution—a wooden baby gate—is cumbersome at best. I thought a decorative metal gate, one that fits securely in the door frame, would be the answer.

Our first stop was Tractor Supply. We needed dog food anyway. While there, we visited the puppies up for adoption; they had just arrived from a puppy mill in South Carolina—a cute mix of what looked like coon hounds, Labradors and beagles. Cooper was drawing attention as well, with one gentleman angling to take pictures with his cell phone. John said it was like having paparazzi stalking us. I'm not sure what the attraction was, but we ignored him and piled a 50-pound bag of puppy food into the cart. And for a dog gate, the salesclerk suggested a pet store in Somerville. On the way there, John suggested we get Cooper off the puppy food, by doing a half-and-half mix. I agreed.

When we entered the pet store, a nasty terrier was making a scene—barking his head off at Cooper. Why would someone bring a dog-aggressive animal into a store? As I turned my attention away from the out-of-control terrier, I saw a young lady crouched down directly in front of Cooper's face, trying to give him what looked like an Oreo cookie in biscuit form. She had rushed right in, without the customary palm-down approach. I asked if she worked there, which she did. She didn't know where the dog gates were, so another salesperson that was more knowledgeable approached. When I told her what we were looking for, she directed us to buybuy Baby across the street. She then turned her attention to Cooper, admiring the poised dog. As a child, she had raised five German shepherd puppies for the Seeing Eye—only one did not pass the test. She had very positive experiences with all five dogs. They were all very well-behaved. There was only one problem—the family had difficulty getting homeowner's insurance. She explained that there is a dog blacklist that is maintained by some insurance companies and, apparently, German shepherds are on it. Though I can understand a company's interest in avoiding risk, but having a well-trained German shepherd should bring your insurance rate down, as it is unlikely that your home will be the target of evildoers.

Realizing that we were off-topic, John redirected the conversation to dog food. We wanted to know which type of food we should move Cooper to, at 14 months. She said, "He's as tall as he will be, but needs to fill out. I would keep him on the puppy food, which contains more fat, at least another six months." Made sense to me. We do have to be careful though. We don't want him to get too big.

Since we had plenty of puppy food in the car, we thanked the clerk for her help and headed to our next stop, buybuy Baby. John dropped me off at the front door, and I had to pass the tempting Girl Scout cookies on display. In hindsight, I would have loved some Thin Mints. Anyway, I was on a different mission. The store had a wide selection of baby gates; I found the perfect one, with metal gate and wooden side panels that match our hickory flooring. Besides looking nicer than flimsy plastic or collapsible wooden gates, this will keep Cooper from climbing the stairs, or annoying anyone who may come to the front door. I should have done this many months ago.

We discovered something very important on the way home. Since John was in the driver's seat, I could actually read the owner's manual for my car. I needed to figure out how to prevent the car alarm from going off when Cooper is left in the car. Since Cooper loves car rides, I often take him on trips to the grocery store, but he has to remain in the car. If I lock the car, Cooper's motion triggers the alarm system. So I've been leaving it unlocked—never a good idea. There is an easy fix though—press the remote door lock twice, in quick succession. This disables the tilt alarm, the feature that activates the alarm if the car moves. That was easy. John was concerned that someone would steal Cooper. Me? Not so much. But now we can be at ease while we shop.

After dinner, which is playtime for Cooper, we took note of his teeth. Plaque is forming. Cooper's teeth had been brushed once by the groomer, but I have never brushed a dog's teeth. Instead, I opt for hard biscuits to do the job.

NOVEMBER 7

Cooper and I joined in our second open-air training session in the park. It's quite the social gathering. We met Diane and her long-coat shepherd Lola. What a small world. Diane is good friends with Cooper's breeder. She learned the grooming trade from her, and now has her own mobile grooming business. Diane had even met Cooper when he was just weeks old. As she talked about her dog, I picked up some new GSD terminology. She calls long-coat German shepherds "coated," and short-coats "standard coat," which is much easier to say, when in the company of GSD owners.

There was only one close call during the entire session. As we practiced figure eights, a dog whipped around and gave Cooper what for. The handler pulled the dog to the ground and yelled, "No!" Cooper didn't react to the unpleasant scene, just inches away. He sat quietly by my side. But the mayhem must have taken a psychological toll. No more than 30 seconds later, Cooper was throwing up. I was able to break the figure-eight formation and take him to a grassy area. We then rejoined the group and finished the exercise. I think that Cooper being the new dog on the block may be to blame. He's not part of this pack…. At least, not yet.

Earlier, a woman who has decades of experience with shepherds had said, "I can tell Cooper is very submissive, so I would keep him clear of any dogs you don't know. He could get hurt." Cooper has never shown aggression toward another dog—at home, at training or at doggy daycare. At this age, it is unlikely to surface. However, if he does get hurt by another dog, that could change.

When we returned home, Cooper enjoyed some down time. While he slept, I called Molly's owners to see if a doggy play date was still on. Indeed, it was. Within the hour, Bob was at the front door. I would swear that Cooper knew it was him. I had said to Cooper, "Molly is coming over!" which caused him to run to the kitchen window, looking for any sign of her coming down the driveway. When Bob knocked, Cooper did not make a sound. I let Bob in, so we could test the new gate that separates the front door from the living room. It was perfect! Bob reached over to pet Cooper, who clearly knew it was play time. With Cooper on lead, we headed to the pen. Susan was standing in the driveway, holding Molly as she began barking. Had she forgotten that Cooper was her littermate? I was taken by surprise; the ruckus didn't appear to affect Cooper in the least. After we slowly introduced them, my tension eased.

Bob says that's the way she plays. It could very well be a male versus female shepherd trait. Before long, Cooper and Molly were playing tag. What a fantastic way to wear a dog out. Racing through the yard, they occasionally collided, but were unscathed. It was comical how they took turns hiding behind the dog house, only to come racing out from one side or the other and chased down. As they played, we exchanged training stories and discussed recent events.

When we talked about CGC testing, I learned something interesting. Susan had tried to get her husky certified, but he failed the brushing test. The evaluator has to be able to brush the dog, without the dog reacting—mouthing or biting. That gave me insight into where I needed to brush up. Even though I brush Cooper daily, he still bites at the brush and my hand. I use the "Stand" command and he does comply— for the most part. Amy and John will also have to brush him, so he gets accustomed to other handlers. That might be easier said than done.

November 8

While reading about CGC certification on the Internet, I located the name of a local AKC-certified trainer, Leslie, who might be able to help me with Cooper's certification. I gave Leslie a call and she was more than happy to help. But since she doesn't have heated indoor facilities, CGC classes will not start until next March or so. We can, however, do private lessons at $65 per hour, a pay-as-you-go arrangement. That works for me. Leslie can meet Cooper and assess his readiness for CGC certification. The best part: Leslie is also an AKC evaluator, so she can conduct the CGC test. We're all set for our first session on the 16th.

November 9

Before Cooper can begin one-on-one training for CGC certification, I needed to pick up a nylon choke collar. I am told that this type of choke collar causes less damage to the fur around the neck. This is coming from a groomer, someone who knows best. I had just switched from a prong collar to the chain choke collar. That is now being replaced by a nylon choke. I could have saved money by going directly to the nylon choke collar.

November 10

Walking with Barb, and Cooper in tow, is a common activity on nice days. The temperature was a bit cold, in the low 40s, but we still ventured out. It's always interesting to see what we'll encounter, chipmunks, squirrels, joggers, bicyclists, neighbors. These are all opportunities to reinforce good behavior. Today, it was a bicyclist heading right at us. Cooper paid close attention. I decided to stop and put him in a sit position. I wanted to see what he would do as the biker passed us. Cooper didn't budge, which was my hope. I praised him and we were on our way. Lunging or barking would have been a problem. Cooper has always been interested in bikers and joggers, no longer in a harmful way, just in a moving-object sort of way.

Cooper's last K9 Nose Work class was tonight. Nothing of interest to note, except Cooper has made a new friend, Sarah, a female German shepherd. She is very sweet and her owner, Loretta, let them greet one another after class. Like me, Loretta has a small dog that doesn't play with big dogs, so we promised to get the two shepherds together.

Oh, and in the interest of keeping Cooper busy, I enrolled him in Level I Rally Obedience, starting on the 30th. I'm not entirely sure what that training entails, but I'll soon find out.

November 11

Our local paper, the Hunterdon County Democrat, reported a very sad event. A 13-year-old boy was with his 92-pound German shepherd, Mongo, when they encountered a 12-point buck in the woods. It's rutting season and bucks are more agitated at this time of year. Mongo had earlier chased this same buck, so it may have been payback time. Mongo was seriously gored and tossed into the South Branch of the Raritan River. The poor boy was hysterical. They wrapped the dog in a blanket and rushed him to the vet. And though people sitting in the waiting room offered to donate their own dog's blood, Mongo died on the operating table.

NOVEMBER 12

The weather was so nice that I had to take Cooper on a social outing. We first hit the bank to cash a check. The teller—a cute, freckled young lady—was pleasantly surprised by Cooper. She hurried through the transaction, then rushed from behind the counter to greet him. As we were leaving, two women admired Cooper, one asking, "Is he a Shiloh shepherd?" I politely said, "He's a long-coat German shepherd, but is often mistaken for a Shiloh." I didn't even know what a Shiloh shepherd was until this spring, when a gentleman in town said, "Look it up on the Internet." From what I've read, the breed is very similar to the German shepherd, but it's not recognized by the AKC. Apparently, the breed founder and a few other kennels separated from the AKC to create this breed, which is recognized by a few rare breed show organizations.

As I moved past other bank patrons, the manager said, "You know, with that look, that floppy ear, Cooper should be a stuffed animal. You would sell millions!" I said, "You think so?" Her response, "Absolutely!" When I asked if she would like to be an investor in any future business venture, I'm not sure I got a response. Anyway, it was a spontaneous and entertaining exchange. Our next stop was the pet store to see Loretta, the owner of Cooper's new friend Sarah.

Loretta's shift was almost over, so we got there just in time. I wanted Cooper to see a familiar face. Other women in the store clearly enjoyed seeing the big dog. One commented on how she had never seen such a large German shepherd. Being his typical laid-back self, Cooper sprawled out on the floor. Loretta came out to say hello to Cooper, and I told her we are going to try for CGC certification. She immediately said, "You should have no problem; he's such a good boy." Her dog Sarah had gotten the certification a few years ago, so she knew the drill. And when I expressed concern over a stranger brushing Cooper, she offered to help. I think I'll take her up on the offer.

While talking about CGC. I asked Loretta why she got the certification. Her response, "Homeowner's insurance." Apparently, if your dog has a CGC certificate, an insurance company is more likely to cover your home. Otherwise, as I've heard on a number of occasions, you run the risk of being denied or, worse yet, losing your coverage.

Before leaving town, one more exercise—chilling for a few minutes on a sidewalk bench. This particular bench faces the door of the town restaurant, so there's a lot of activity. As one restaurant worker passed by, he looked down at Cooper and said, "Gorgeous dog!" just as a woman and her young daughter stopped to talk. This little girl was adorable. I had her extend her hand to Cooper, and then let her pet him lightly on the head. After that visit, we sat for a moment more. I wanted to see how Cooper would react to the gentleman about to ride off on his motorcycle. Cooper has seen Greg coming and going on his cycle, and the noise can be deafening. Only eight feet away, as the man kick-started the cycle, Cooper swung his head around. There was no attempt to flee, hide or bark.

NOVEMBER 13

Today was prep day for our dinner party tomorrow. While chopping vegetables, I watched as Cooper launched into a barking frenzy on the patio. That was unusual, so I popped my head out the door. As Cooper was looking skyward, I realized what the fuss was all about—a hot air balloon was slowing passing by; they are very common in our area. I stood next to him, watching. The barking stopped. Whenever Cooper sees something that unnerves him, I say, "Check it out." It can be a hubcap on the side of the road or a mailbox, anything new. This gives him the confidence to investigate, not fear. I know of a dog that can hear a hot air balloon approaching from a half-mile away,  barking and shaking in terror. If I condition Cooper now, this might be avoided. In fact, I'll give him treats next time. That should calm his rattled nerves, as the swooshing of propane burners come and go.

After cooking and cleaning tasks were checked off the To Do list, I went golfing with Jane, my neighbor. On our way to the course, we talked about her childhood, growing up with German shepherds—five in all. Remembering how protective her father's dogs were, she chose Labradors when she married and raised her own family. Over the last 25 years, she's had four black Labs. Only one had a mean streak, acquired later in life. But despite that one dog, she continued to adopt Labs, avoiding, as she said, "A huge headache." I suspect that raising three boys was challenging enough. Having to keep a close eye on a shepherd was not part of the plan. Knowing that shepherds require extensive training, if you aren't prepared for what lies ahead, she said, "Get a Lab." I felt compelled to tell Jane about the stories I've heard over the past year about Labs that have bitten people. I later learned that there are 75 million dogs on this earth. And checking statistics from the Center for Disease Control and Prevention, there are nearly five million dog bites annually. Dogbitelaw.com reports that two percent of the U.S. population is bitten every year. Sources vary, however, regarding which breeds are the most likely to bite. It appears that the pit bull terrier, Rottweiler, German shepherd and Doberman pinscher top the list. But drilling deeper, you can also find statistics that show smaller breeds—Welsh corgi, chow chow, Chihuahua, lhasa apso and others—are even more likely to bite. Obviously, the small breeds do far less damage. The bottom line is that every dog needs training, regardless of breed and size.

NOVEMBER 14

Today's test: a dinner party with family—eight people in all. Once again, Cooper proved himself to be a good dog. I am always on alert that someone coming through the back door could alarm Cooper. But he has proven that he knows what *is* and *is not* acceptable. Today, I simply held tight to Cooper's collar as we went down the basement steps. I'll admit he partially dragged me, after hearing unfamiliar voices. As we approached the guests, I put Cooper in a sit, but with no cause for concern, I released my grip. He mingled with everyone. That went well. In fact, during appetizers and dinner, Cooper simply napped at our feet. Even without having walked him, he was content. At one point, John said, "Cooper was never really a puppy," a reference to the fact that this big dog is so easy-going.

NOVEMBER 15

As I worked in my office this afternoon, I heard a muffled thud on the floor below. Cooper was in the kitchen. Why didn't he bark? I went to check on Mom. Her bathroom door was closed. I called out, since her hearing is poor, "Are you okay?" I asked if she was hurt. To my relief, no broken bones. At just 4'10", there is not much distance between her and the floor. This has been to her advantage and as she jokingly says, "I appear to be able to fall without doing any damage." Let's hope that continues to be the case.

In preparation for tomorrow's visit with Leslie, the AKC-certified dog trainer, I had John brush Cooper. I use the "Stand" command, which was part of Level II Obedience training. As John took the brush, he stood there without turning to mouth John's hand or the brush. Having stood nicely for John, Cooper was rewarded with a biscuit.

NOVEMBER 16

I learned about a large-breed health issue from a *Meals on Wheels* volunteer—bloat. When she came to the door, I could immediately tell she was not intimidated by Cooper. She was calm and direct, remarking on his size. She's had four shepherds over the past 20 years; one was even from Cooper's kennel. Very knowledgeable, she told me to <u>never</u> allow him to run and play after a meal. That can cause bloat, which is more common among larger dogs, particularly deep-chested breeds like German shepherds, Doberman pinschers and Great Danes. I had heard of this malady, but knew very little. To the Internet I went. The technical name for bloat is Gastric Dilatation-Volvulus (GDV), a condition that is the second leading cause of death among dogs, after cancer. Anyone who owns a big dog should research this condition, as it has a 50-percent mortality rate and can kill in less than one hour.

After bidding the MOW volunteer good-bye, I raced out of the house with Cooper. We had a noon appointment with Leslie. Halfway there, I realized I had forgotten the directions. With no time to waste, I went from memory—which is never good—but we got there at 12:00 p.m. sharp. Since so much hangs on this evaluation, the last thing I wanted was to be late. We greeted Leslie in her well-appointed barn, complete with framed AKC certificates and ribbons adorning the walls. Her first question, "Shiloh shepherd?" I get that a lot. After a few minutes of chit-chat, we got down to business. Retrieving her notes on CGC requirements, we ran through the steps an evaluator would take to test a dog. It is really quite involved, as I learned from the exercises on the AKC website. It encompasses everything from basic obedience to less structured components, like the evaluator running past the dog.

Cooper excelled in a few areas—sit, down and stay. I put him in a sit, dropped the leash, and walked 10 feet away. Bolting through the open barn door was an option, but he remained focused on me. The recall was flawless, with Cooper trotting back to me and sitting. Leslie then took Cooper and had me leave the room. She said that many shepherds have a hard time with the separation exercise. I was concerned since Cooper is so attached. When I handed the leash to the trainer, I held up my palm and said, "Stay." I then proceeded into her office. Leslie allowed a minute to pass, though three is the official requirement. I stood silently behind the office door; Cooper could not see me. There was no whimpering or barking. Things were going well. When Leslie said, "Come on out," she was impressed. Cooper was still sitting nicely at her side. Wow! She said, "Give him a treat. He's a good boy!"

Where we had trouble was walking at heel. This can be a struggle. The evaluator wants to see a loose leash, with a large u-shape, not a taut line. We needed help. Cooper does not follow my lead or watch my movements. He's just forging ahead. I had to get his attention focused on my eyes. That's where clicker training will come into play. Leslie gave me a clicker and will be forwarding instructions on how to use it.

Another problem area she detected was Cooper's response to having his legs touched. This is a test that indicates how the dog reacts in a vet's office. Every Canine Good Citizen has to allow the vet to examine any part of its body—no biting or growling allowed. Cooper didn't bite or growl, but he was reticent, as indicated by his clenched jaw. When he's relaxed, he's panting, with tongue on full display. Here, he was yawning. Though his yawning wasn't excessive, it was a sign that he was trying to relieve stress. Leslie suggested I recruit strangers to handle Cooper's legs, while I feed him treats, so he realized that good things happen when he is being handled. This holds true for the vet's office as well. She believes you should give your dog treats throughout the office visit. I will follow that advice from now on.

Next, Leslie checked Cooper's reaction to someone running past him, back and forth. I left the leash loose as she ran past Cooper. He did follow her, but in a non-aggressive way, almost as if to play. That included mouthing her hand. She stopped and said, "Wait." I immediately said, "Did he mouth your hand?" He had. I told her he tends to mouth our hands and arms, as we play. She repeated the exercise again, and he did the same thing. Never clamping down, just pressing his teeth to her hand. It didn't appear to be a problem. I explained that we have never corrected this behavior. (At home, we say, "No bite," when his mouth encases our arm or hand. But I did not mention this because the word "bite" would be negative. Cooper has never bitten us or anyone else. And since I've been told that shepherds are "mouthy," I choose to not make a big deal out of it. Like our goldens, he may just grow out of it. And for Leslie, she didn't see any aggressive tendencies during this exercise.

To test Cooper's behavior with other dogs, Leslie was about to get her dog when I asked if she would brush Cooper. I was curious how he would do. Though I brush him often, how would he react to a stranger? I handed the brush to Leslie. She passed it over the length of his back, twice, and that was that. He stood nicely, and I tossed him a treat. No problem there.

Now for the dog aggression test, Leslie asked that I take Cooper into her office. She brought out Jackie, a 9-year-old Australian shepherd. A well-trained dog, no doubt, Jackie was placed at one end of the barn, off leash. When Leslie said "Okay," Cooper and I entered the barn. Cooper was at full attention, eyes firmly fixed on Jackie. He strained to get closer, but I held him tight. Leslie and Jackie, Cooper and I needed to pass one another, without Cooper lunging or barking. Cooper wanted to sniff Jackie in the worst way. No aggression. The next test, how he interacted with Jackie while he's off-leash. I don't think this part is in the CGC test, but it gives her some idea about his temperament. Cooper just sniffed Jackie, which she was trained to tolerate. Leslie rewarded her dog as she was subjected to Cooper's inspection. All went well, as Cooper soon turned to the bag of treats sitting on a chair.

Before leaving, I asked what she thought about CGC certification, and she indicated that it shouldn't be problem. But I have to work on heel and start clicker training. Initially, every time I click, Cooper gets a treat and I say, "Yes," in approval of the behavior. I'll then tie that activity to looking at me. If he looks at me, I click, and he gets a treat. Soon, he should be watching me and then we'll work on heeling, so when I make a turn, he stays right with me. Otherwise, he's just bumping into my leg, which won't look good during the formal test. As for being handled by strangers, I may take him to the pet store and recruit someone there.

I also learned something else from Leslie. If your dog lunges at another dog, the offender should not be forced to the ground in a position of submission. She considers that the old way of handling the situation. I was surprised by that. I've watched as dogs were corrected in that fashion. Leslie believes it's best to ignore the behavior. I should give the recipient of that aggression treats, while saying "Good boy!" This will reinforce his non-retaliatory behavior.

LESSONS LEARNED

✔ Choke collars are for training purposes only; they should never be left on a dog otherwise. And there are many different types of choke collars. We've moved from a prong-type choke (that trainers don't like) to a chain-type choke. The goal is to move to a nylon choke collar. The benefit of nylon, according to a groomer, is that it will not carve away at Cooper's fur.

✔ Clicker training is a form of operant conditioning, which has gained popularity as a gentler training method. The principal behind clicker training is that you reinforce good behavior, which the dog (or any other animal) will tend to repeat. I know of one family that used clicker training to acclimate a rescued 7-year-old Weimaraner to a toddler. In just one training session (with a professional trainer), the dog was associating the child with good things—treats. But don't try this at home; consult with an expert. For more information on clicker training, visit *www.clickertrain.com/whatis.html.*

✔ While on walks, a dog may lunge for squirrels and chipmunks. Don't get caught off-guard. When Cooper spots a creature, I say, "Leave it!" This includes passing cars and bicycles.

✔ There are two good reasons to get Canine Good Citizen (CGC) certification for your dog. First, it may help with an insurance company that is reluctant to provide homeowner coverage. Second, if you take your dog on vacation, and stay in a hotel, they may ban shepherds; an allowance may be made for a CGC-certified dog. Any dog can be CGC-certified; AKC registration is not required.

✔ The practice of brushing a dog's teeth has gained traction in recent years. It's a good habit to maintain a dog's oral hygiene, but I don't see myself getting on the bandwagon. So in lieu of brushing, I give the dogs hard biscuits twice a day.

✔ If you live in a rural setting where you share space with deer or bears, be extra vigilant about supervising your dog's outdoor activities—just as you would a child. A family's beloved shepherd was killed by a whitetail deer buck. Bears and coyotes have also been known to maim or kill dogs.

✔ A gate separating a dog from certain areas of the house, for instance, dining room and foyer, is a smart move. The collapsible wooden baby gate, the type you have to release or step over is a pain. Install a baby gate that allows you to pass through. The sides are held to the door frame by screws or pressure. It's well worth the money. Now if Cooper gets to the front door before me, there's a buffer zone.

✔ A shy puppy, as Cooper was, is not necessarily a bad thing. In one professional trainer's experience, the outgoing puppies can present more training challenges. Her past litter of puppies included a shy female, which she held onto for another few weeks to do more socialization work. It was that very dog that went on to achieve success in obedience competition.

✔ A German shepherd club is another way to socialize your dog, while you meet people with the same interests. Check with the AKC for groups in your area (*www.akc.org*).

✔ Hip dysplasia, which plagues large dogs, can be exacerbated by a severe slope in a German shepherd's back. Cooper's back does not taper as much as other dogs I've seen, but he does have a tendency to drag his back paws, which can be a sign of trouble ahead. All we can do for Cooper, as he gets older, is maintain a healthy weight.

✔ A dog that stares at another dog may prompt an attack. It's best to keep your dog clear of others, unless you know for certain that there are no aggressive tendencies.

✔ To diffuse a dog-on-dog confrontation before it occurs, for example, in a training session where one dog clearly does not like another, face your dog in the opposite direction; allow no more eye contact.

✔ The "Enough" command should be used to stop a dog from doing whatever he's doing, like barking. Cooper isn't a big barker, but a number of shepherd owners have said that their dogs did not start barking in earnest until they were two years of age, which is also when the guarding instinct kicks in. Setting limits now, by command, will really help down the road.

✔ In public, people should ask permission to pet your dog. Besides being common courtesy, it can prevent a person from getting hurt.

✔ Bloat (Gastric Dilatation-Volvulus) is potentially very dangerous, so never allow a large dog to engage in vigorous play right after a meal. Bloat is more commonly seen in larger, deep-chested dogs, like German shepherds, Doberman pinschers and Great Danes. For information on bloat, visit *www.aspca.org/pet-care/dog-care/dog-care-bloat.aspx*.

✔ Family members should take turns feeding the dog. This tells the dog that leadership in the pack can be held by people other than the primary handler.

Month 14:
Positive Developments

"It's said that people get the dog they deserve."
—Linda Wisniewski

November 18

Cooper was a real menace this evening—snatching chicken bones from the kitchen garbage, tissues from the bathroom trash, knocking a glass of grape juice onto the living room rug. This is uncharacteristic behavior, and may be Cooper's way of saying he needs to get out more. The weather has been lousy—rainy and very windy—so outings have been limited. We did, however, practice clicker training; Cooper catches on quickly. When he looks at me, I click, he gets a treat. This will get him looking to me for instruction, a precursor to loose-leash heeling.

After settling in for the night, I realized I hadn't seen Meeko all day. I called him from the porch, where he usually scales the fence to greet me, meowing all the way. I called and called. Checked the garage, barn, anywhere he might have gotten trapped. When Amy got home from school, I had bad news—no Meeko. Since he's still learning the ways of the outside world, I was not hopeful; red-tailed hawks circle over our property every day. As I was losing hope, John said,

"Did you check the garden shed?" Wouldn't you know, he was trapped in the shed. He was eager to make a hasty exit. When I carried him into Amy's bedroom, the delight on her face almost made me cry. As annoying as that cat can be, we really do love him.

NOVEMBER 19

Cooper spent a half day at doggy daycare, something he thoroughly enjoys—I think. He drags me into the place, so that must be a good sign. I find it fascinating that they tell us that Cooper is one of the very few dogs that checks for his collar and leash, which they leave in his very own cubby hole. He'll suddenly stop playing to go check that it's still there. Play can then resume. Perhaps that gives him comfort in knowing he wasn't abandoned.

But as enthusiastic as Cooper is to visit daycare, he is equally excited when I pick him up. Like most Fridays, Stephanie was handling Cooper; he loves her. In fact, when I asked to take a picture of the two of them, Cooper licked her face. I've never seen him do that. As hard as I try, he won't lick my face. Some might think that's a good thing, but I want Cooper to replace his tendency to mouth my hand and arm with a lick, so I use "Kisses" as the command; doesn't work so well. But, today, Stephanie got Cooper's oversized tongue across her cheek multiple times. We then chatted about Cooper's progress in daycare and how she considers his temperament "middle of the road," where I had considered him submissive. She said if play in the yard gets rough, he just walks away. No aggression, just avoidance. In other words, he doesn't just cave to the other dogs by flopping on his back, which I would have expected.

Stephanie just adopted a young male German shepherd from working blood lines. Named Bogey, Stephanie adopted him from a family that didn't think it was fair to keep a "working dog" in a pet household. In just 10 weeks, she's made amazing progress with him. She said that it's critical for a high-energy dog to have a job, so she and Bogey are involved in search and rescue training. We were also talking about how some people don't understand the commitment you must make when bringing a German shepherd into your home. Using me as an example, she said, "Look at all that you've done

for Cooper." She's right. Hands down, this has been the most demanding—but also the most rewarding— experience raising a dog. Anyone interested in bringing a German shepherd into their home needs to consider their intentions. Will the dog be an integral part of the family, with consistent daily training, or left to entertain himself? Having gotten wrapped up

in this discussion, I almost forgot to pay Stephanie. As I handed her the money, a dozen dogs behind the door began howling in unison, as if to say, "Stephanie! Come back!"

Our next stop was the pet store. I had called Loretta before leaving the house to see if she was working. My plan was to see if Cooper would let her handle him, especially his legs. I was glad to see that no customers were in the store; Loretta and the store manager were there. As we approached them, Cooper looked a bit unsure of himself, stretching his neck to sniff them both. I explained how the leg-touch test didn't go too well; Cooper clenched his jaw when Leslie handled him. The store manager then approached Cooper and kneeled down in front of him, then with reassuring words, asked him to shake. He obliged. As she handled his leg, she kissed his paw—a brave move, I would say. I quickly fed him a new treat—dried lamb lung. Yuk! I almost forgot that you have to associate the physical intrusion with something positive—food. Cooper eased up, and began taking treats from Loretta. As long as Cooper doesn't retreat or growl, I think we can work through this. I would just hate to fail the test on this one point.

Making our way back to the car, we paused so I could take a picture of the damage done to the historic, 140-year-old steel bridge in town. A woman had lost control of her car and crashed into a main support beam—right before the holidays. Merchants must be in a panic. As Cooper and I stood there, a middle-aged woman in a late-model Porsche Boxster stopped her car, opened her window and yelled, "What kind of German shepherd is that?" I answered "Long-coat…with a floppy ear." Her response, "I had one just like that. Massage the ear." I said, "Really?" Her comeback, "Worked for me!" She then drove off. I can't make this stuff up. It really happened. As we made our way back to the car, I thought about all of the effort I put into Cooper's ears. Who knew massage was the answer? Forget the curlers, tape and glue, Knox gelatin, cottage cheese, even Breathe Right nose strips. I should have simply arranged for a canine masseuse. On the bright side, I've discovered that Cooper's floppy ear prevents him from completely blocking my view of the television.

NOVEMBER 20

Two stops today, Tractor Supply and Home Depot. Tractor Supply was the same old routine, with Cooper trotting alongside the shopping cart. What we saw on the way out stopped us in our tracks. A burly man, well over six feet tall, was holding an English bulldog puppy in his huge arms. I had to meet this puppy. Based on its size, I suspected he was just five to six weeks old, nowhere near what he said—twelve weeks. Its eyes were barely open. Cooper strained to sniff the puppy's paws, but I kept a close eye on him. Would he see this tiny object as a possible snack? To the contrary, Cooper was soon bored.

On to Home Depot…. The mission was to find window locks for the barn. Every time we enter this enormous store, I expect an employee to rush up and say, "No dogs allowed!" It never happens, so we just said hello to the greeter and proceeded on our merry way. Today, I needed to ask the greeter where I could find locks. We must have stood there for half an hour, as people began gathering around Cooper. Three older women circled in front, which I thought might ruffle Cooper; he just sat there, as each reached out to pet him. As that is going on, I spotted a large boxer coming toward us. Despite the fact that boxers look intimidating, in my experience, they are really nice dogs. This boxer, named Sophie, was no different. What a sweet disposition. Of course, I did first ask, "Is she friendly?" The woman responded, "Oh, yes." I still wasn't so sure, but Sophie and Cooper sniffed up a storm, with not a single warning sign. We later ran into the pair in the lock aisle. Again, we stood talking, as the dogs weaved around one another. I welcome any opportunity for Cooper to meet a friendly dog.

As we finally reached the checkout counter, a woman approached, asking, "Is that a Williams dog?" My stupid answer, "No. It's a long-coat German shepherd." I soon realized she meant Kelly Williams, the Hawk Point Kennel owner. I explained he was out of a kennel called Valley Crest. As she left, a Home Depot employee made a huge fuss over Cooper. I was trying to scan the window locks at the self-checkout, but had to wait as a full-grown man placed his face directly in front of a dog with enormous teeth. As soon as he left, what approached us? The Home Depot mascot, in a costume I can't describe. It wasn't a clown, just a huge figure that I've never seen before. Cooper just stood there. Thankfully, he didn't linger long. I would not have blamed Cooper if he were afraid, but there was no reaction. To think I have two more years of socialization. It's mind-boggling.

When we returned from the store, I put Cooper in his pen. For the next few hours, he would have to take a back seat. I was going to watch my very first hockey game. Amy's friends play on college teams in New England and the games are streamed live on the Internet. I connected Amy's faster laptop and clicked the link she sent, logged in with my zip code, and was soon watching the action. What a nice diversion from *The Cooper Project*.

After 32 years of marriage, I only recently realized that John is a germaphobe. Not really. But Cooper will visit the water bowl during playtime, leaving us with soggy toys to throw. So I guess I can't blame John. It is gross, but I suck it up and toss the rope or ball, whatever is of interest at that moment. John will toss Cooper a few peanuts, a nightly ritual. And now when he tosses peanuts to Ozzie, in the interest of fairness, Cooper has matured to the point where he no longer snatches peanuts from his little, but older, brother. He just turns his head back to watch when the next one might be coming his way.

NOVEMBER 21

Cooper and I attended our third GSD training in the park. I had seriously considered giving this activity up, since other dogs seemed to not take kindly to Cooper's presence. I'm so glad that I threw caution to the wind and went back. Giving it

another chance was the right move. There were no close encounters. Perhaps the other dogs were beginning to accept Cooper.

When Cooper and I spotted Diane and Lola on the opposite side of the parking lot, we made our way over. Cooper and Lola get along nicely. I explained to Diane that I'm working on Cooper's CGC certification, and how he may not pass the handling exercise. She stepped right up and began schmoozing with Cooper. She ran her hands over his back and down his legs without hesitation. Cooper was fine. Since Diane is a professional dog groomer, she understands canine body language and there was nothing to indicate that Cooper would not accept her getting up close and personal. What the CGC evaluator wants to see is that Cooper is not reactive when handled. Though Diane had success, we still need to work on this requirement.

Later in the session, as I stood between two seasoned dog handlers, they assured me that I'd get hooked after taking Cooper to Rally Obedience class later this month. They may just be right. Cooper is eager to please; I just haven't found a treat he cannot refuse. I've gotten away from greasy hotdogs, but need a substitute.

Since the weather was so nice, I took Cooper into town. Our destination: the pet store. The streets were bustling, people and dogs everywhere; the perfect setting for socialization. Standing in the pet store, Cooper met no less than 30 people, young and old alike. It was kitten adoption day, so the place was packed. A gentleman soon engaged me in conversation by saying, "Your dog reminds me of my wolf hybrids." Is that a compliment? Oh well, I took the bait. He was a professional photographer who also ran a wolf rescue facility in Arizona some years ago. It was an amazing story. After our rather lengthy chat, he recommended that I read a tried and true dog training guide— *Good Dog, Bad Dog*. I had actually read the book back in the 1980s; a refresher couldn't hurt. Another recommendation he made was to wean Cooper off of his treats. Preferring praise, he said, "Cooper will look to the pack leader for approval, not food." While this may be true, it goes against Cooper's AKC trainer's advice. Leslie said to reward Cooper whenever meeting someone new, at the vet's office, during formal and at-home training sessions—anywhere and everywhere. Positive reinforcement will remain a part of our plan.

Before we left the store, I delighted in Cooper's ability to be so very gentle with the kittens. One young lady looked concerned, as she cradled a tiny fur ball in her arms. Looking up at me, she said, "Is he okay? Will he bite?" With the size difference, I understood her apprehension. My response, "Cooper has a cat at home, so he knows better." I should have said, "Cats rule, dogs drool."

Stepping out of the store, directly in front of us stood a dog I had only read about—a Labradoodle! This was my very first opportunity to greet this strangely beautiful creature. A cross between a Labrador retriever and standard poodle, it was a very approachable dog. When we got closer to the young owner, I said, "Hi. Is your dog friendly?" Without hesitation, she exclaimed, "Oh, yes, he has been through a year of 4-H training." Her enthusiasm for her dog, also named Cooper, was contagious. And sensing that my Cooper was comfortable, I loosened my grip on his leash. They then greeted one another in the customary fashion. They were fine, so the young lady looked up and said, "He's even bigger than my dog!" The young lady's father then emerged from a nearby store. Alongside him was a puggle, a pug and beagle mix. Two popular "designer

dogs" in one place; it was a Kodak moment. Looking back, Cooper proved himself again; he mingled nicely with both dogs and cats.

NOVEMBER 23

With *Meals on Wheels*, it's always someone new at the door—someone Cooper can potentially frighten. But today he met his match, a woman who paid no attention to him. She marched right in, while extending her hand for Cooper to sniff. I gave her a biscuit, which she handed off to Cooper. All was good. He was sprawled at her feet while we talked for over 20 minutes about her rambunctious Bernese mountain dog and golden retriever. These volunteer visits have been a blessing in disguise. Cooper is consistently challenged to keep his cool. If people rarely came over, it would take far longer to calm the savage beast.

NOVEMBER 24

The day before the big events—the 18th Annual Turkey Trot and Thanksgiving—Amy was busy prepping for the 5K race. A regular runner over the past four years, Amy is in perfect form. She trains on steep hills, while the race is on level ground. That will bring her in around 27 minutes, for the 3.1-mile course.

Cooper joined Amy on her run, which I realized was not advisable until he was older, but I couldn't refuse. Afterward, they both took a ride over to the Center for Educational Advancement (CEA), the not-for-profit that coordinates the event. She had to pick up her race package, a t-shirt and number. As she and Cooper entered the building, they were held back by the large crowd. She asked workers near the door if she could bring Cooper in. A woman said, "Yes, but stay by the door." This didn't make any sense, since Amy had to stand in line, so she went with the flow. Two little girls were soon drawn to the big dog; each stood as tall as Cooper. Cooper licked one of them. He's not a big kisser. But it's all good. Last year at this time, a close encounter like that may have frightened him.

NOVEMBER 25

Thanksgiving Day! This year was different than last; I prepared many of the dishes yesterday. This allowed me to join Amy, John and Al at the Turkey Trot. There were over 5,000 people registered for the event.

Bundled in warm clothes, we all piled into my car, with Cooper jammed into the rear compartment. We found the perfect parking spot, right behind Stryker's Paint Store—a business John has frequented for over thirty years. Making our way through the crowd on Main Street, I stopped everyone for a photo in front of the historic Flemington Court House, where the Lindbergh Trial was held in 1935. We then bid Amy farewell and she trotted off to the start line.

Music was blasting, a real party atmosphere. And as we strolled along the street, numerous people were drawn to Cooper. One woman was astonished to see the dog of her youth, a long-coat, black and tan German shepherd, complete with floppy ear. You could tell she was thrilled to see the incarnation. And while we passed within inches of spaniels, terriers, retrievers, and mixed breeds alike, there wasn't one ill-tempered dog among them.

After the race, which took Amy about 27 minutes—a very good time—we were headed for home under a light snowfall, which, thankfully, held off until the race was finished. From door-to-door, the event took less than two hours. Before long, we were greeting Greg and his family, Al, Stu, and later Debra, my childhood friend, as we all gathered together for the Phillips Feast. Cooper mingled like a pro. Perhaps he was in party mode as well. He didn't make any untoward moves when people entered the house. Of course, that bowl of biscuits is a permanent fixture at the back door.

NOVEMBER 26

I talked to Sandy today, the wife of the building contractor John subcontracts for. She has a three-year-old Belgian shepherd (Malinois), Maggie, that she rescued. She often laments that the dog only responds to her husband and that she needs to do more socialization. In fact, she offered to drop Maggie off at my house for training, which got a good laugh. Seems Maggie is not so good in public settings, and disregards her commands when they are outside in the yard. If Maggie breaches the perimeter fence, it's a challenge to get her back, so they have been begun using an e-collar. Despite some difficulties, in terms of obedience, she said Maggie is a great family dog—loves the grandkids. Her son, not so much.

NOVEMBER 27

A very cool, windy day. Despite the weather, Barb, Cooper and I went on our 2-mile walk. As we reached the base of Pine Hill Road, we are stopped in our tracks. Cooper's and our eyes were fixed on the commotion at the end of the bridge. A dark SUV was stopped on the Franklin Township side of the bridge. We watched as a young man was dragged around the rear of the car. Then, the rear door opened and someone inside the car pulled the guy into the vehicle. This took all of about 10 seconds, after which the doors slammed shut and the car accelerated. It bottomed out on the other side of the bridge and sped through the campground. Barb and I high-tailed it back up the hill. When a car approached from behind, Barb checked to see if it was the SUV. We were unnerved by what we had seen. I then called police dispatch to report what we saw. In New York City, they have a See Something, Say Something campaign. Ignoring what we saw was not an option. Clearly, this could have been kids fooling around, but if someone's child turned up missing, I would never have forgiven myself. After calling the event to the attention of the police, we were visited by an officer. John yelled, "The police are here! You reported an abduction?" As to whether I was reporting an abduction or not, it was what it was—someone had been forced into a car, not of his own free will. The urgency of the matter required that I immediately appear in the kitchen. After just getting out of the shower, I threw on a top and sweat pants; no brushing one's hair at a time like this. The officer needed to respond to this report, in the event that an Amber Alert had to be issued. I explained what Barb and I witnessed, and then dialed Barb's number. She spoke with the officer. He got both our contact info and left.

After everything settled down, I asked Amy how Cooper responded to the officer entering the kitchen through the basement. The stairs were once a trigger point. How would he handle this without me in the room? She said he did bark, sniff and growl at him, but the officer never looked his way. This was an interesting test because I was not there to place myself physically between the visitor and Cooper. John and Amy were in charge. Cooper was not entirely comfortable with the agitated officer, clearly on a mission, but he did not misbehave. (As for the outcome of a possible abduction, I read nothing in our local paper; no news was definitely good news.)

NOVEMBER 28

Today was Cooper's fourth GSD training session in the park. There were 14 dogs in attendance—quite a sight. We went through our paces, but Cooper was dragging. The trainer said he didn't like his treats enough to cooperate. I ran to my car and got the dried lamb lung. That did the trick.

Between exercises, a woman told me her dog, Blaze, is developing bad habits. He bit her friend twice when she entered the house. I referred her to Cooper's trainer, Steve. After that conversation, when all of the dogs were in a down-stay position, the instructor had a friend skipping in a weaving pattern through the dogs. The hope is that your dog will remain in position. Just two dogs from the end, the volunteer was bitten; Blaze had lunged and nailed her in the leg, only inches from Cooper. The woman was quick to respond, and pushed Blaze to the ground, yelling and striking the dog. I don't agree with this harsh treatment, but it's difficult to know how you would react in the heat of the moment.

After training was over, Diane and Lola stopped by the house; Cooper could romp with a dog his own size. When we brought the dogs into the pen, and let them loose, Lola was naturally hesitant, even snapping at Cooper. But they soon worked it out. Cooper was running circles around his new friend, as he tried to engage her in a game of tag. She did a few laps with Cooper, but mostly stuck by Diane. As long as she didn't attack Cooper, I was happy and so was he.

NOVEMBER 29

I had been vacillating on whether or not to register Cooper with the AKC, since we did not intend to show or breed him. Since I had procrastinated, it cost me an additional $35, for a total of $55 to get a slip of paper with his name on it—Super Cooper of Stoneledge.

NOVEMBER 30

Every day brings new events in Cooper's life. Today, contractors were expected around 8:00 a.m. I was ready with a supply of biscuits in my pocket. Only one problem… Peter, the General Contractor, walked right in the back door. I had a grip on Cooper's collar as we descended the steps, but as we rounded the corner, Cooper barked twice and growled. I put Cooper in a sit, and then Peter approached. It all happened very quickly so though I handed Peter a biscuit, Cooper was still unsure of this person. Another gentleman appeared at the door, but there was no fuss; Cooper was focused on Peter. I released Cooper and he followed me up the stairs, while the men surveyed the job site.

Later, as Peter and I stood in the kitchen, Rob, his business partner, walked through the door. Cooper dashed over to him, but didn't bark or growl. Rob was confident in his stride, completely ignoring the dog. It amazes me how a dog can read body language, in this case a calm, assertive person.

After the contractors left, it was time to take Amy's car in for service—another opportunity to let Cooper mingle. Sitting in the service center lobby for two hours meant lots of attention for Cooper, new noises, and people coming and going. Cooper preferred to face the door, keeping an eye on things. He appeared perfectly comfortable, sniffing people; most would then gently pat him on the head. For the most part, Cooper was content to lie beside me, which was a pleasure. One patron commented on his quiet temperament. I was sure to reward that calm state of mind.

Tonight's Rally Obedience class—our very first—was challenging. Of the 10 or so dogs and owners, we were the relative newcomers; all but one other person had already gone through the class. I was listening closely to Cheryl's instructions. She set up stations throughout the room, each with a ground-level sign giving the handler a command. For example, the sequence of signs read:

1) SIT & DOWN, 2) DOWN, 3) HEEL SLOW,
4) HEEL NORMAL, 5) SIT, 6) SIT & TURN RIGHT,
7) WEAVE IN/OUT (of cones), 8) TURN LEFT,
9) SIT/DOWN/SIT, 10) EXTRA PT. SIT —
    ADVANCE — HEEL TO SIT.

Of the wide variety of dogs in class—a Basset hound, Australian shepherd, sheep dog, Bernese mountain dog and springer spaniel—the pug named Ruby was the star. Having raised a Shih Tzu, I never thought a small dog, with an equally small brain, could perform so well. When it was my turn to run the course with Cooper, it was a semi-disaster. Completely uncoordinated, I dropped Cooper's treats at one point. I had to remind myself that it's all about having fun.

Cheryl mixed up the signs for the second run-through:

1) SIT/DOWN-STAY, 2) DOWN, 3) 360 DEGREES
RIGHT, 4) SIT/DOWN (circle around dog to heel
position), 5) 360 DEGREES LEFT (I blew this one by

going right), 6) STOP/SIT — FRONT — STEP to Right or Left (bring dog to front).

December 1

I should have my head examined. I'm seriously considering another German shepherd—a female. Cooper's Rally Obedience trainer knows of a woman in New York state that might be a source for a pup. I know nothing about their breeding program, but plan to make an inquiry. Maybe by next summer, we'll have a new addition to the family. In fact, when I ran this plan by Amy, she enthusiastically said, "I'll help!" Though I was tempted to make a joke about the likelihood of same, I held my tongue.

This afternoon, Cooper and I had our second, and last, CGC lesson with Leslie. This session, we focused on loose-leash walking/heeling. We practiced baiting Cooper with treats. The only problem: he was much more interested in her treats than mine. What did she have stashed in her pocket that made him so attentive? She had Cooper heeling like nobody's business. When my turn came, I was all thumbs, holding the leash, the treats and clicker. I just couldn't pull it together. She suggested I forget the clicker for now. Good advice. That allowed me to focus Cooper on the treats as I was walking. When my supply ran out, Leslie gave me the coveted treat—all natural, dried chicken strips with special herbs, no preservatives. Cooper was now looking at the treats in *my* hand as we walked, which is what we want. When I stop, and he sits, he gets the jackpot—a whole bunch of treats, as a motivator. We looped through the barn at least five times until we got the hang of it. My goal was to have Cooper under complete control, without the need to pull on the leash, which Leslie said just nags the dog. So he must respond to my physical and verbal commands. Promising to work on this, we moved to handling. Could Leslie place her hands on Cooper without his showing any expression of discomfort or fear? Last time, Cooper had clenched his mouth. This time, he was fine. She ran her hands across his back and down his legs. There's only one problem—for the Canine Good Citizen evaluation, her husband would most likely be handling Cooper. I have a feeling that a stranger may unnerve the dog. Another concern is whether or not Cooper will pull me after spotting another dog. Leslie uses her Australian shepherd, Jackie, during testing. Cooper wants to get to her in the worst way. How do I keep him from pulling me toward another dog? Before leaving, I asked if we could again test Cooper's ability to handle physical separation. I went into her office, out of sight, as she stood with Cooper. Unlike last time, when he didn't make a peep, he made a slight fuss. This was probably due to Jackie being in the room with me. He yipped and whined, but nothing over the top. When I returned, after the full three minutes, I rewarded him. Leslie said that his behavior was fine. He sat down, as if to say, "Okay, I get it… she'll be back."

DECEMBER 2

Cooper and I had to remove some items from the bank safe-deposit box. As the manager was helping us, I asked him if he had ever seen a dog inside the vault. He paused a moment and then said, "Come to think of it, no." As he leaned down to place his key in the lock, Cooper sniffed the long box as it emerged. Though confined in close quarters with a stranger, he was curious and perfectly comfortable.

Next stop, the car wash. Cooper has been through the car wash many times over the past 14 months, enough so that he was now at ease. When he was a puppy, the flapping leather strips pounding the car, spinning brushes, and spray jets had him nervously looking through every window. It must be frightening, from a dog's perspective. From my perspective, it's just one more experience in my quest to make Cooper comfortable in any environment.

DECEMBER 4

Cooper and I took our second trip to the Motor Vehicle Inspection Station. We had just gotten Amy's car inspected a few days ago. Today, it's time to inspect the pick-up truck. New Jersey did away with full mechanical inspections last July, so now they just test for emissions. Cooper was in familiar territory. As we pulled up, the MV official approached the driver's side window. When he spotted Cooper, he took two steps backward, as if startled, and said, "Wow!" I assured him Cooper was friendly. As I handed him my paperwork, he said, "Put the car in park, remove your belongings… and take the horse with you." Dogs aren't allowed in the heated waiting room, so we stood outside in the bitter cold. As we took our position at the end of the building, a man waiting for his car immediately approached, saying, "What a beautiful dog!" As he was kneeling, getting right into Cooper's face, I quickly handed him a biscuit. Even though Cooper is unlikely to bite anyone, it still unnerves me when someone rushes up. Having treats at the ready makes me more comfortable and, by extension, Cooper.

DECEMBER 5

A relatively quiet day, having gotten home in the wee hours after a thoroughly enjoyable Andrea Bocelli concert at the Prudential Center in Newark. In fact, Cooper's only outing was to Dominick's Pizza. Otherwise, he whiled away the better part of the day in the yard, watching John stack firewood. Periodically, John would enter the pen to race after Cooper, who plays a mean game of soccer ball keep-away. We really blew it when it came to teaching Cooper to fetch. Oh, sure, he will bring the ball back, but just out of reach, turning on a dime to prevent you from grabbing hold.

Cooper and I practiced loose-leash walking later in the day, only without the leash. Those dried chicken strips really get Cooper going, prancing obediently next to me, almost reading my mind as I loop through the kitchen and living room. With Cooper in heel position, I enthusiastically said, "Let's go!" The treats are secured in my left hand, held to my stomach. Whenever Cooper looks at either the treat or me, he's rewarded. He's adept at reading both my facial expressions and body movements. And most miraculous of all, he can do a left-side heel. When he's sitting directly in front of me, I circle my left hand counter clockwise, bringing him directly to heel position. I honestly don't know how he picked this up. Trial and error I suppose. If he comes in crooked, I straighten him out and pop a treat in his mouth. It takes repetition. I cannot wait to try this in Rally tomorrow night, when the pressure is on. At least, I now have a treat Cooper cannot refuse. With his undivided attention, we'll do far better.

As Cooper finally rested tonight, I noticed something: Cooper and Ozzie often sleep next to each other, almost as if Cooper is using Ozzie as his lookout. If anything is amiss, Ozzie often hears it first. Since Ozzie's sight is very poor, maybe his hearing is more acute.

Ozzie, however, would not have been of any help earlier in the night. Cooper spotted an emerging threat—Mom moving ever so slowly, and silently, on her power chair through a dark hallway. Cooper stood in the kitchen growling. I couldn't imagine what was upsetting him. When I realized it was just Mom's silhouette in the dark, I had him follow me down into

the master suite, turning on the lights as we made our way. Soon he could see the source of his distress. As a dog bred to guard sheep, this behavior is desirable. In the context of our home, I would not correct him. He's doing what comes naturally, protecting his flock. I did, however, encourage Mom to flip on the lights. In fact, maybe I should reattach those bells, so she jingles all the way.

DECEMBER 6

Cooper and I were in the middle of a training session when Amy arrived home. While I had Cooper in a stay, he was far too excited about seeing Amy, so he broke loose. I didn't correct him. It's a joy to watch those two together. Cooper is pretty unflappable until Amy gets home. Even Ozzie was spinning in circles. Once order was restored, I couldn't wait to show Amy how Cooper heels off-leash. I'm particularly proud of his left-side heel, from front position. Amy was impressed.

DECEMBER 7

Cooper's second Rally Obedience class was much like the first. With only an hour and 10 participants to run through their paces, there's a lot of down time. Cooper just sleeps. You would think that watching the other teams practice would pique his interest, but boredom appears to set in. He only comes alive when the trainer says, "It's Cooper's turn!" On our first exercise, weaving around cones, I tripped over the last cone; the crowd broke into laughter. How embarrassing. I'm undoubtedly the class klutz. After correcting my mistake, we finished the exercise without further incident. That was, of course, until our second time on the floor, when I misread a sign. Actually, I don't think I even read it. I was to have Cooper swing left and heel. I had him swing right. Cooper was nearly flawless. I was not. In fact, when we first arrived for class, I showed Cheryl how good Cooper was at left-side heel. I only wished I had taught Cooper the "Swing" command but he understands my hand signals. I really don't even need a verbal command. If we stick with this, we may become proficient enough to compete one day.

DECEMBER 8

Amy's 24th birthday! Where did the time go? After opening cards, stuffed with cash and lottery tickets, we headed over to Snap Fitness; we're joining for the winter months. Unfortunately, we missed the morning window of opportunity. I'll have to stop by tomorrow. What a pain. Speaking of pain, John is prepping for his first colonoscopy tomorrow.

DECEMBER 9

I had to fulfill my promise to Amy and join the gym. Since I preferred to join in person, versus on-line, I grabbed Cooper's leash and off we went. Would the gym allow a dog into the facility? I was apprehensive about this excursion. Keeping Cooper in circulation is critical, yet I may be pushing my luck. I threw caution to the wind. The worst they can say is "No dogs."

Before reaching the gym, we stopped to say hello to two women in the parking lot. I scrounged biscuits out my pocket and handed one to each. They asked if he was some breed that started with an L, so I'm suspected Leonberger, a breed that can resemble a long-coat shepherd. After exchanging pleasantries, we entered the small strip mall. Since the gym locks its doors, I had to wait until someone noticed us. When the manager appeared, I asked, "Is it okay to bring him in?" He said, "If he's well behaved." My reply, "Oh, yes." And Cooper was the perfect gentleman as the manager gave us a quick tour. While we signed all the obligatory paperwork, Cooper laid quietly at my side. As we left, I was so glad I had brought him along.

Before we could leave the building, a well-coiffed woman sitting in the hallway, perhaps a salon employee on break, gave

Cooper a sizable chunk of roast beef, right out of the middle of her sandwich! That was a first.

Since the gym trip went so well, I decided to bring Cooper to the Ford dealership to drop John's van off. I needed some information about local auto body shops, so it was the perfect excuse to bring Cooper to the counter. There was an interesting mix of reactions. One young man proudly showed me pictures of his German shepherd and Doberman pinscher, each taped to the bottom of his computer screen. He then asked if he could take a picture of Cooper to send to his girlfriend. Cooper sat nicely as he captured a cell phone image. Patrons, however, were not so thrilled about sharing the tight quarters with a large animal. I didn't give Cooper any slack on his leash. I've learned to read people pretty quickly, sensing who's receptive to a dog and who is not.

December 10

Last night's weather included heavy rain, which neither Cooper nor Ozzie are fond of. But what's nice, since Cooper is

not a water dog, he rushes outside to my "Hurry up" command and does his business faster than any other dog we have owned. Unlike Ozzie, who goes in endless circles, Cooper gets right to it.

While Cooper has a keen understanding of whatever I ask of him, like doing his business in an expedient manner, I did make a recent mistake. I allowed him to climb onto the ottoman, thinking it was cute. He now thinks that lounging on the adjacent loveseat and sofa is permissible as well. I guess he can't distinguish an ottoman from a sofa. When I've caught him lounging, I just say, "Off" and he obliges. From now on, no more ottoman!

DECEMBER 12

John and I enjoyed another trip to Tractor Supply with Cooper. Before reaching the store entrance, we had to stop and greet a woman and her very energetic yellow Labrador puppy. Though Cooper towered over the pup, the little one was thrilled to meet him, dashing all around the big dog. We then entered the store only to run smack into another yellow Lab puppy, only this one was much younger. People were gathering to see the tiny puppy and enormous German shepherd greet one another. I wish I had brought my camera along. With socialization behind us, we focused on our shopping. Still, people were turning their heads, saying, "Beautiful dog!" as we weaved through the aisles.

With the cart full of bird, chicken and dog food—100 pounds worth—we proceeded to the check-out line, which was unusually long. That gave Cooper a lot of time to commune with people, the very reason for his presence in the store. Two little girls—maybe five and six years old—couldn't take their eyes off of Cooper. They peered out from behind their parents' legs, as we crept closer to the register. Finally mustering enough courage, they began waving dog toys in front of Cooper, who was only mildly interested. I kept a close eye on the activity, since Cooper and the girls looked eye-to-eye. Exposure to little children is really what Cooper lacks, so this encounter was excellent. The girls were very respectful, and only before leaving the register area did one of them reach out to pat Cooper on the head. John thought Cooper looked very comfortable today, which hasn't always been the case. I agreed. But then John promptly ran over Cooper's tail with the cart, not once, but twice.

DECEMBER 13

Construction began on the kitchen. The very best carpenters are on the job, Peter and Rick. There's only one problem, Cooper will have none of Rick. Ever since he dumped two cords of wood, directly in front of Cooper's pen, the dog has been spooked. Even a year later, Cooper growled when he entered the rec room and no biscuit offering would do. After the peace process failed, Cooper retreated to the kitchen, barking at the top of the stairs. I didn't press the matter and like Leslie suggested, I ignored him. Later in the day, Peter and Cooper got along just fine. It appears that Cooper's early, negative experience has created a lasting memory of Rick, the guy who rattled his cage, literally.

Later in the evening, John—in a rare reflective moment— remarked on how beautiful Cooper is, saying, "Look at that coat and fur around his neck. Someone might steal him." Uncle Tom had expressed the very same concern. I'm not sure if such a threat was real, but I find comfort in knowing that Cooper had a microchip ID embedded between his shoulder blades.

DECEMBER 14

Second day of construction and Cooper's settling in for the duration; there's no need to make a fuss over diesel pick-up trucks pulling in and out of the driveway, and continuous banging and crashing. It's all good. However, I thought it best to take Cooper with me while I ran errands. One stop was the ophthalmologist's office—to inquire about eyeglass repair. Cooper and I got an immediate welcome from the receptionist Susie. She came right up to Cooper, presented her hand, and then lavished him with affection. She was very enthusiastic about her love for shepherds and quickly pulled out her cell phone, snapping a few shots. The picture was for her boyfriend, who also loves this breed. I said, "Let me take a picture of you and Cooper." She didn't hesitate. Later, I asked if she had ever

had a shepherd. She had, as a child. Her parents put the dog down after it bit a police officer. Bad form indeed. Their next dog was a cocker spaniel. As we were leaving the store, Susie announced

to an elderly couple coming through the door. "Hello! This is a service dog, Cooper. He's in training." While it is doubtful Cooper will ever go into service, he is certainly in training.

After dinner, Cooper and I braved an arctic blast to attend our third Rally Obedience class, which was much the same as last week, just a different course to run. As Cheryl explained each station, I momentarily thought, "What am I doing here?" It seemed far too complicated. But after watching the experienced handlers take to the floor, my comfort level grew. As we waited our turn, Cooper just rested, until Cheryl called his name. Jumping to our feet, we did our best to follow the signs. No real slip-ups this week....at least laughter didn't break out. That's not true. When Cooper was given the sit, down, sit, down sequence of commands, he chose, on the last down, to shake instead. When I said, "Down" again, he handed me the other paw. At that point, I was laughing. On our second and last run, he was flawless. Cheryl even said he handles the tough stuff well.

During down time in Rally, which is probably 50 minutes of the 60-minute session, I was snapping pictures, mostly of two magnificent Bernese mountain dogs. Both females, they

have wonderful dispositions. Their owners said they have never seen an aggressive Bernese, and they have attended shows with hundreds of dogs—all of the same breed. When I floated the idea of getting a Bernese puppy, John promptly shot me down. "Our house is too small," was his answer. When I mentioned that one of the women in class has two Bernese in her townhouse, he was not swayed.

DECEMBER 15

As people came and went with their Christmas gifts and cards, I realized that the post office is a great place to socialize a dog. Cooper met five very nice people—all dog lovers. Cooper accepted their overtures, but in his own reserved way. No tail wagging from this dog. No aggression either. In the very tight space of this rural post office, he was up close and personal with everyone who walked through the door. Only one woman didn't reach out to pet Cooper. She simply stepped over him to reach her P.O. box. Looking down, she said, "I could never bring my shepherd here. She would bite someone." I asked, "How is she at home?" Her response, "She's very protective, and if someone comes into the house and appears uncomfortable, she picks up on it immediately." Cooper is much the same, which is all the more reason to keep him in close contact with the outside world.

DECEMBER 17

The book I ordered, *Good Dog, Bad Dog,* arrived today. The section that has breed-specific information was of particular interest. I had to differ with one statement in this book. Specifically, the text read, "Anyone can own a German Shepherd Dog." The book does go on to say, "Aggressiveness can be an inherited quality in this animal." That being said, is it safe to say that anyone can own this breed?

Barb gave me a tour of her son Chris' home, which is undergoing major renovation. He's made tremendous progress. As we went from room to room, Cooper's nose was in overdrive. As we descended the basement stairs, Cooper froze on the landing. Perhaps he smelled traces of the many bichon frise dogs that once inhabited the home. It was the first time I had ever seen Cooper shake; his back legs were quivering. It may have just been the loose stair treads. I didn't press him any further.

LESSONS LEARNED

✔ A dog that can't burn off steam is likely to acquire bad habits, like running through the house with reckless abandon. Indeed, bouncing off the walls can take a toll on your furniture, carpeting and wood floors.

✔ There are places other than pet food or big box stores that are dog-friendly. My rule of thumb: if the establishment doesn't sell food or fine china, why not? The worst thing that can happen is they ask you to leave.

✔ Have everyone and anyone handle the dog, including petting, brushing and handling its legs and paws. This is something that should start on day one.

✔ Daily brushing has more than one benefit. Besides helping to keep loose hairs under control, my frequent brushing of Cooper's long hair has gotten him accustomed to grooming. The battles of yesteryear are behind us.

Rally Obedience is a relatively new activity for dog owners. The Association for Pet Dog Trainers (*www.apdt.com*) developed Rally as a way to promote positive relationships between dogs and their owners. Any dog can participate–pure breeds, mixed breeds, even disabled dogs. There are three levels of difficulty and titles can be achieved in each.

✔ If you don't allow the dog on the couch (or bed), don't allow him on an ottoman; he can't distinguish between the two. That just comes down to being consistent with the rules.

✔ Begging can always become a problem behavior. I try to avoid this by limiting Cooper's food to his bowl, or treats while he's in training.

✔ Rather than buy new dog toys, I rotate them. When Cooper tires of the current toy supply (strewn throughout the kitchen and living room), I recapture his attention with one pulled from the cabinet.

MONTH 15:
GOOD DOG!

"There's no such thing as a difficult dog,
only an inexperienced owner."

—*Barbara Woodhouse*

DECEMBER 18

I think John is getting jealous of Cooper. He lamented this morning about how Cooper has his own bed, his own shelf in the pantry. "He has it better than me," he said. I assured him that wasn't the case, but *The Cooper Project* is wearing thin on John and Amy. "If you're not talking about Cooper, you're watching Elf or Animal Planet. Animal Planet, yes, but Elf? That movie is a family tradition this time of year. Besides, I only watched it once.

Later, when John heard Molly was coming over to play with Cooper, he got testy, saying, "Play dates with dogs are all fine and good, but we need to get the construction debris to the dump!" I appeased him by helping throw the carpeting into the pick-up truck, but Molly would be here any minute. They had not played together in weeks, so I was happy for Cooper. When they arrived, Bob let Molly loose, though only after the warm-up period where Molly is held on-leash until she gets comfortable. Within minutes, she's set free and the chase was on. I then turned to Bob and said, "Brandy's loose-leash walking (down the driveway) looked really good." He still had to correct her twice, but she would comply. He and Susan have done a lot of leash training, which is still a struggle for me when walking Cooper. Bob was also working with an e-collar to correct Molly's tendency to bark while riding in the car. (They only undertook this measure after consulting with a professional dog trainer.)

The blustery winds had us frozen to the bone, so we called it quits. Bob had a package for Cooper, so I followed them to their car. Susan had put together a gift bag for Cooper, a Christmas present for hosting the play dates. It was an unexpected surprise and much appreciated. I'll let Cooper tear into it on Christmas. Before leaving, Bob also showed me the e-collar, with two prominent electrical prongs that go against the dog's neck. Since he said it doesn't hurt, I asked him to try it out on my arm, which he did. It was a tingling sensation, nothing more. At that setting level, it's just to get the dog's attention.

DECEMBER 19

We've once again enlisted my brother Greg, the architect, to help lay out the new kitchen. I wasn't home, so when Greg heard Cooper barking at the door, he waited for John. Good move. In the past, the guys just marched right on in. Not anymore. Cooper wants to protect the house, which is his job. Once John greeted Greg, Cooper quickly calmed down. In fact, he would not leave Greg's side, as long as he was handing out biscuits and throwing bologna sandwich fragments his way.

DECEMBER 20

For the second time, Cooper met Frank. With the kitchen renovation in full swing, Frank is installing sheetrock. Frank first met Cooper when he was just three months old. John and I were chatting with him outside his apartment. He looked down at the cute pup and asked, "What's his name?" John said, "Cooper… Amy named him after BMW's MINI Cooper." Frank's response, "After four years of college, that's all she could come up with?" Since Frank is a true animal lover, always with biscuits in his pockets, I tried to not take offense.

An unexpected sighting today: a man and his German shepherd at Walmart. Rarely do I see dogs in that store. Since they were standing in the checkout lane, I pulled up behind, though other lanes were shorter, I had to learn about this dog. He was talking to the woman in front of him, so I listened for an opportunity to strike up a conversation. As his dog came to greet me, I said, "Is he an Hawk Point shepherd?" To my surprise, he said, "Yes." What I learned from this exchange was that a dog needs service dog credentials in order to enter the store. I asked if those credentials come from the AKC, but he thought the ADA (American's for Disability Act). I'm not so sure about that, so I later called Walmart to determine what credentials are required. The clerk she said you need documentation to state the dog is for service purposes. She sounded rather unsure of herself, so I'll have to do some more research. I also learned that the gentleman, Chris, and his dog, Jimbo, used a trainer in Hopewell who specialized in German shepherds. Chris also said that he took Jimbo everywhere, even a Bruce Springsteen concert. That's certainly taking socialization to the next level. Since his dog is 18 months, I'll have to ask Diane if there's any chance that Jimbo is a littermate of Lola. That would be quite the coincidence. Chris said his dog was great with his three kids; the only time he isolated the dog was when he's eating. As Jimbo rested near the grocery bag carousel, you could tell he was an unflappable dog—much like Cooper. As the dog stood up to leave, the cashier came from behind the register and gave the dog a kiss on the top of the head. That's a trusting soul. As she began ringing up my items, Chris dug out his BlackBerry to show me his trainer's phone number. He then shook my hand; we wished each other "Good luck" with our dogs. I only wished I had asked him to come meet Cooper, who was in the car, but that would be an imposition.

DECEMBER 21

Another trip to the post office, and another German shepherd story…. The patron behind me patted Cooper on the head, telling me how her brother has a shepherd at his industrial roofing business in Trenton. "The dog is terrific with people, but not with other dogs," she said. The dog apparently has it in for the dachshund across the street. On the flip side, the dog is great with kids and people. And when it comes to loyalty, this dog takes the cake. Unbeknownst to the owner, the dog followed him up a 12-foot ladder, only to take a nasty fall. I dreaded what the woman would say next, but it was good news. The dog was not seriously injured. John also fell from a 12-foot ladder, only he spent three days in intensive care, with broken ribs and three fractured vertebrae. He, too, bounced back.

Cooper was such a good dog at Rally Obedience class. He didn't even flinch when a woman clunked him in the head with her plastic chair as she moved it (and her dog) to the other side of the room. I turned to look at the woman on my right, as if to say, "Did you see that?" No reaction. Only after class did I realize that she must have been making space between her dog, an energetic Bernese mountain dog, and Cooper. Until tonight, there was a barrier separating my seat (and Cooper) from the other class members. We were now seated side-by-side. He spent the class lying only inches away from Helen and her seven-pound Pug, Rosy. As handlers and their dogs ran the course, Cooper paid no mind. When it was our turn, we didn't do so badly. In fact, Cheryl complimented us after we executed a Level II maneuver—an opposing turn where I went left and Cooper went right, an about-face. Cooper also excelled at another high-level routine where the dog must stand while the handler moves away six feet. Cooper needed to stay in that position as the judge (Cheryl) passed her hand across his back. I then circled around him to heel position. Having not moved a muscle, Cooper was the only dog to follow the commands. If we take Rally again, we might be ready to move on.

December 22

I'm considering giving Amy an animal deterrent spray for Christmas. She already thinks I worry too much. But as a jogger, it's not outside the realm of possibility that a dog could attack. If a dog is in pursuit, I understand that the jogger should stop, turn in the direction of the approaching dog, and cross their arms. A moving object, with flailing arms, must be too tempting to a dog that is looking to make trouble. That said, having a powerful citronella canister at the ready couldn't hurt. It's not much of a gift though; I think I'll unveil it at a later date.

Picking up Cooper at doggy daycare gave me my very first glimpse of him playing with the other dogs. The pack of 40-plus dogs is generally out of sight. Today, probably due to the

brutal wind and bitter cold, they were indoors. All I could see though the office window and door was Cooper racing after a Labrador—back and forth. I only note this because Cooper has gone from a reserved puppy to a more confident, happy dog. I attribute that to once-a-week doggy daycare, as well as consistent socialization. The daycare owner remarking on how Cooper "plays with everyone," which is nice to hear. What I used to take for granted with goldens—a love of everything—has only been achieved with Cooper through consistent exposure to the world.

DECEMBER 23

When people see a German shepherd, it often conjures up stories from their past. Take the story told by our electrician, Dave. He recounted how his neighbor's German shepherd, King, was often left in the backyard tied to a zip line—not a good idea. An even worse idea was to put a choke collar on the dog. As fate would have it, the dog got loose. Despite King being AWOL, the owners still went on vacation, enlisting Dave to be on the lookout. Dave did one better and looked for the dog for five days straight. He found him in thick brush, wrapped tightly around a tree; the dog was unable to lie down or quench his thirst in the stream just a stone's throw away. The choke collar was snagged on a branch. To free the dog, Dave lifted his 90-pound frame to remove the collar. Once free, King headed for home.

The old kitchen counters are no more. Dating back to the 80s, it was time to go. When all is said and done, we'll be up to code. We're lucky to have Peter and Rob on the job today; truly the best of the best. As the men broke for lunch, and Cooper and I were headed out to do some errands, Peter caught me by surprise. He said, "How about bartering the last three days of labor for your designing our website?" Taken aback, I said, "Are you sure?" His response, "Is that fair?" "More than fair" was all I said. This would help trim costs off the project. A welcome development. Peter's final words, "Merry Christmas!" I thought, "And how!"

DECEMBER 24

Christmas Eve and construction is on hold until after the holiday. Peter and his wife Sandy did, however, stop by to drop off some building supplies and a dozen fresh eggs from their farm. Before we showed Sandy the work in progress, she had to first meet Cooper. Sandy loves shepherds, and has one of her own. Having come prepared, she pulled treats from her jacket pocket, one by one. Cooper was doing anything to comply with her commands to sit, shake, down, but he wouldn't crawl. I tried to teach him that trick, but without success. At some point the conversation turned to Cooper's earlier troubles. She had thought Cooper may have bitten her husband. I was startled by that revelation. Not wanting to panic, I just made my way into the room where John and Peter were talking. When I got a chance, I said to Peter, "Did Cooper ever bite you?" He said, "No. Cooper never bit me." It must have been a misunderstanding. I was just relieved that the intensive dog training and socialization hadn't gone down the drain. We then continued with our tour of the new space under construction and the barn, with Cooper our constant companion.

DECEMBER 28

Amy and I hit the gym early today, and then got pizza for lunch. Something's wrong with that picture. Afterward, we stopped home to clean up and head back out, this time with Cooper. With a record-breaking snow having kept us in for days, poor Cooper must have cabin fever. We stopped at the bank; Amy took Cooper in while I did my banking. Next, the optometrist. Amy had to help me pick out new eyeglasses. Since Cooper had been welcome there before, I thought nothing of bringing him along. How wrong I was. The optician saw us coming. As we entered the store, she quickly said, "He can't come in unless he's a service dog!" My comeback…. "We were here last week without a problem." She asserted, "The doctor is in and we have patients today, so out of concern for them we can't have a dog in the office." Amy looked at me and said, "Told you so," like she was scolding a child. I imagine she was embarrassed; she was holding Cooper's leash. I handed her the car keys and they made an about-face. This is only the second time, since Staples, 10 months ago, that Cooper was unwelcome.

I later dropped Amy off at Walmart; she needed cat food for Meeko. Oh, the money we spend on pets. Since Cooper's visit to the optometrist was a bust, I parked the car and brought Cooper to Walmart's front entrance. We hadn't been back since Cooper's close encounter with a pit bull. Within 30 seconds a young lady stopped her cart, asking, "Is he a German shepherd?" I said, "Yes." Everyone really does have a story. Her father was a police officer in a K9 unit. Not fond of his 130-pound German shepherd, she recounted how the dog attacked her brother's girlfriend. I asked, "Did your father keep the dog?" He did. That same dog would later bite him, twice.

DECEMBER 29

As I sat in the kitchen this morning, it hit me. We were placing the new kitchen sink in the wrong spot. It was only 7:30 a.m. and I'm vacillating—do I talk to Peter, who had just pulled in? I gathered the courage to descend the steps and ask those in the know—the contractors. Peter said, "Yes. You have enough room to shift the sink over." Peter then reminded me that his wife Sandy had made that suggestion on an early visit. He was right! I'm no architectural genius. Sandy had planted a seed that suddenly germinated after the old cabinets had been removed. It opened up such possibilities. Good thing we were all in agreement, as four plumbers arrived only minutes after a major design change. And just as the room filled with tradesmen, Cooper bursts through the plastic barrier, which was supposed to keep dust out of the house, and climbed over a five-foot pile of lumber to get to me, oblivious to all of the men. This dog is only happy when he's by my side.

DECEMBER 30

Not since John burned Amy's baby bottles on the stove some 23 years ago, have I been so terrified. I was still sleeping as my weary brain seemed to be saying, "I smell gas." I dismissed the thought as just a lingering odor from the construction crew's power tools. How wrong I was. John awoke and went to investigate. What he found downstairs was a kitchen and living room filled with smoke. At that very moment, the smoke alarms went off, in unison. I ran downstairs, where I met Amy; John was headed to the basement. With the kitchen renovation, there was no telling what happened. I was yelling "Call 911!" John said, "Wait!"

With my eyes burning from the acrid plumes, I sought relief on the patio, with Cooper and Ozzie right behind me. At 15 degrees outside, that didn't last long. When we returned, John said that smoke was billowing out of the furnace; he hit the emergency switch. What had happened? His best guess, the furnace filter had become clogged with construction dust and debris, even though plastic barriers were in place. Amy headed back to bed, as did I. John stayed behind to open all of the windows and connect portable fans. As I lay in bed, unable to fall back to sleep after the sudden surge in adrenalin, I thought of those stories about the courageous family dog that sounds the first alarm. Cooper and Ozzie must have taken the night off.

-2011-
JANUARY 2

It was a warm day for January—the upper 40s—so Cooper and I attended the Sunday training class in the park. With the holidays, we had missed the past few weeks. In that time, Cooper had perfected his left-hand (swing) heel, so I was hoping to test his skills in the great outdoors. Before the session began, we were witness to a frightening scene. Buddy and Trevor, two long-coat shepherds were entangled in what looked like a fight to the death. Neither handler could separate them. All I could make out was Buddy tearing at the left side of Trevor's neck and ear. Once the trainer seemed to pry Buddy loose, the dog immediately clamped down on Trevor's left leg. From my vantage point, it looked like Trevor's leg would be broken. As she pulled with all her strength, she didn't know his leg was still in Buddy's mouth. When they were finally separated, Trevor was wounded. I just hoped that it was nothing serious. Sometimes fights sound and look worse than they are. Tracy looked Trevor over; the leg appeared okay. She did find puncture wounds and abrasions on and under his ear. This gentle shepherd was bleeding. One woman scrambled to find antiseptic in her car, but turned up empty. I had a first aid kit in the car, which I quickly retrieved. Tracy applied antiseptic to the wounds. The session began soon thereafter, though the atmosphere was markedly less cheerful.

When it was time to practice recall, the trainer hooked Cooper up to her 20-foot lead, while telling me that her sister's cat is named Cooper. I asked, "What breed of cat?" She said, "Maine Coon." I told her that my mother and I once bred and showed Main Coon cats. Anyway, I had to get back to work, and put Cooper in a sit-stay. He complied. In fact, he performed the recall exercise like a champ, coming to front position, and then swinging out to my left for a perfect heel. We even gained praise from Bonnie. I said, "We've been working on that." Her response, "I can tell!"

After training, I had the chance to talk with another shepherd owner. She had brought along her 6-month-old shepherd, Ben. This dog appeared to have some dog aggression issues, so we kept our distance. After a few too-close encounters, I've learned. But this woman was very knowledgeable about shepherds, so I listened intently while she described her first shepherd, some 25 years ago. She had brought home a beautiful 8-week-old puppy only to find he was terrified of everything. When her husband first laid eyes on him, the puppy backed into a corner and growled. The dog had never been socialized with people during those first critical weeks of life. The vet predicted that he would turn into a fear biter, and said that he would probably end up putting the dog down. Though the breeder offered to take the puppy back, this woman would not accept defeat. Instead, like me, she took the dog everywhere. Intensive socialization, specifically, daily trips to the mall, made the difference. The vet would later show the dog to people in his waiting room, singing the dog's praises. She had even achieved Canine Good Citizen and Companion Dog titles. So what was initially considered a lost cause was anything but. That was the type of happy ending I like to hear.

Cooper's day was not done. We picked up John and headed to Tractor Supply. As we walked into the store, I said, "We're going to get your food, Cooper." To our amazement, Cooper led us directly to the dog food aisle. This shouldn't surprise us; he's one smart dog. We then went to Lowe's to look for a new washer and drier. Cooper has never been in this store. Do they allow dogs? We passed by two greeters flanking the entrance. We were good. But Cooper appeared to annoy the appliance saleswoman, as we were repeatedly interrupted by people stopping to meet Cooper. It is remarkable how a big dog can stop grown men in their tracks.

JANUARY 5

Our fifth Rally Obedience class was dedicated to learning about the Companion Dog Sports Program (CDSP), which requires a dog to run through a set sequence of exercises, at the direction of a judge. This program is unrelated to AKC-type obedience events. Of course, Cheryl had us attempt the novice exercises which consisted of on-leash heeling, off-leash figure eight, moving stand for an exam, recall over a bar jump and honor sit-down, where the dog must remain in place as another team runs the course. Each exercise, if successfully completed, is worth 40 points, for a maximum of 200 points. If the dog fails any one exercise, you are eliminated, so it's rather difficult. Cooper, for instance, decided to run around the jump rather than over it. He wasn't alone. But after getting a feel for this activity, I thought it easier than Rally Obedience.

Throughout this class Cooper has sat next to Rosie, the adorable Pug. At no time was there any animosity between them, until tonight. As Cooper was lying there, with his head resting on the floor, Rosie approached, as her owner said, "You like him, don't y--" But just as the word "you" was to leave her lips, Rosie lunged at Cooper. It happened so fast. But Cooper's only reaction was a low growl; there was no retaliation on his part. He didn't even get up. I told him, "Good boy," and tossed him treats. Time to go home. Oh, and Cheryl did tell us that CGC testing will be held at her facility on January 16. I'm hoping that Cooper will be ready by then.

JANUARY 6

I've been procrastinating on getting my car in for service, so I bit the bullet. It'll be a whopper of a bill! Since Amy's car needed a minor fix, she followed me in her car. Of course, Cooper was not to be left behind. He sat with me for over two hours, until we were finally told they would need to keep the car. But over those hours, Cooper met at least a dozen people. Amy later recalled how one man stopped and said, "Oh, what a substantial nose you have!" Talking to this gentleman, who was smitten with Cooper, I later learned that his wife doesn't like dogs. What a shame. He could hardly take his eyes off Cooper. When I finally learned what the repair costs would be, the service representative looked down at Cooper and said, in a very low voice, "He makes me sad." I said, "Why?" Three years ago, he had to part with his female German shepherd due to signs of aggression toward his baby. As he searched for his BlackBerry, I thought he was going to show me pictures of the baby. Instead, he showed me pictures of the dog, a whole series. You could tell he loved her very much. She looked much like Cooper, only a smaller, standard-coat version. Just a few days ago, the dog had to be put down. Not for aggression, but complications from an intestinal disorder.

Cooper is due for booster vaccinations, most importantly, rabies. I can't get his license from the town without a Certificate of Vaccination. This was another two-hour wait. We took it in stride. Cooper continues to amaze me in what was typically a very stressful environment for our goldens. In contrast, he

lies down, places his head on the floor, and watches events unfold around him. He hardly even picked his head up to acknowledge two inquisitive miniature pinschers and a Lhasa-poo, named Rocky.

With a fearful Jack Russell and a flatulent bull dog across the way, Cooper made me proud. When we finally entered the examination room, he was apprehensive. The last time he saw Dr. Reynolds, a rectal exam was performed. That would make any dog quiver. But we got his weight, still 80 pounds. He hasn't gained any weight since October 24, despite our best effort to help him pack on a few pounds. Dr. Reynolds, like most others I've spoken with, said,

"You want him to be on the lean side." When fully mature, he is predicting that Cooper will run about 100 pounds. After he examined Cooper's ears, eyes, teeth, and heart, his assistant—who is very skilled—trimmed Cooper's nails. He was not fond of this, as most dogs are not, but there was no protest. And other than one evasive move toward the door, Cooper hung in there. This all bodes well for the upcoming CGC testing.

JANUARY 11

Our last Rally Obedience class! Much of the same—two times around the course, with my continued reliance on Cheryl to prompt me through some of the signs. Overall, Cooper did well. He's particularly adept at stay, down, sit and come. With continued work, I'm hoping that we could compete in a Novice Rally trial. That hope was later tempered by Cheryl's conclusion at the end of class. The upshot: Cooper's not a Rally dog. He's admittedly slow, so since Rally is a timed event—you must complete the course in less than four minutes—Cooper would need to quicken the pace. I accepted her assessment and asked where we should go from here. She suggested repeating Obedience Level II, with new people and dogs. I agreed.

I then spoke to Nancy, seated next to us. Daisy, it turns out, was entered in an AKC Obedience and Rally Trial this weekend. I wanted more information, but the woman seated next to her leaned way over, as if to get my attention. She points directly at Cooper, who was lying quietly by my side and said, "Is his ear ever going up?" It's almost as if she were itching to ask that question for the past six weeks. My response, "Nope. That's it." While many follow up their ear inquiries with something to the effect, "It gives him character," she had nothing further to say, as if disappointed. On that note, Cooper and I left the building, stopping only to give Nancy my e-mail address, so she could send information on the AKC event.

JANUARY 12

Another snow storm had John shoveling the driveway at 5:30 a.m. Perhaps one day he'll throw in the shovel and hire a plowing service. Since contractors were not expected due to the storm, all was quiet in the house. To make the most of the day, John and I set out to choose kitchen fixtures and flooring. Of course, Cooper came along. Our first stop: the plumbing supply store. I hesitated to bring Cooper in, so we could easily move about the store. I'm not sure how the topic came up, but our saleswoman learned that Cooper was in the car. She demanded that we go get him. As John went to get Cooper, she proudly showed me pictures of her own dogs. An enthusiastic dog lover,

she took one look at Cooper and was all over him. She even insisted on my taking him off the leash. Against my better judgment, I set Cooper free. He followed us into the faucet showroom, but his circling around wall-mounted glass sinks got me nervous.

Would "You break it, you bought it" apply here? Rather than take chances, I corralled the curious canine and could once again focus on the task at hand—picking out faucets. But in the process, dog war stories were intermixed with product details. At one point, she stopped in her tracks, turned to us, and said, "I didn't want to mention this but three German shepherds attacked my dog, ripping a hole in his hindquarters; it took two major surgeries to repair the damage." I was astonished that anyone would have three shepherds running loose. Anything could happen when dogs form a pack. But she faults herself for having her dogs off leash. The costly encounter was resolved through the court system and the shepherd owners paid the price.

At Home Depot, Cooper knows the drill. Up and down the aisles we went, in search of floor tile. We hit on the perfect material—Tuscany Gold porcelain. Picking up samples and a few other things, we headed to the checkout. The woman at the register rushed from behind the counter to pet Cooper. I gave her a biscuit. That scene always reminds me of being at a petting zoo. Thankfully, Cooper wasn't the least bit hesitant. We've made some very real progress. After the woman scanned our items, she returned to Cooper's side, leaning down while saying, "So nice to meet you. Good-bye now." Dogs really do bring out the best in people.

JANUARY 13

I'm going to take the plunge and register for Canine Good Citizenship (CGC) certification. There's probably no better time. Cooper is constantly exposed to different people and places. Why wait? So I e-mailed Cheryl to ask for the evaluator's name and phone number.

After dinner I called the CGC evaluator, Renee. Looks like it will be a busy schedule, with over 20 dogs registered for CGC and therapy dog certification. At first, I thought we might be turned away. But when she learned that Cooper was a German shepherd, she took an immediate interest. Shepherds are one of her favorite breeds, having owned and worked for many years with shepherds in AKC obedience events.

When I asked if she had any advice for test day, she recommended coming to the site 15 minutes early, so Cooper could get acclimated. We will definitely do that. Most importantly, I have to remain calm, as she noted that Cooper will pick up on my state of mind and react accordingly. If I'm nervous, he'll be nervous. In fact, I might combat the test-taking jitters by running him through his paces in the park on Sunday morning. Oh, and I cannot forget to bring along Cooper's rabies vaccination certificate and his AKC registration number. John just put the new license tag on Cooper's collar, so we're good there. Don't want to be turned away on a technicality.

JANUARY 14

John learned first-hand how German shepherd stories abound. Our plumber, Tony, who is working on our kitchen renovation, has a shepherd that suddenly began attacking their Welsh corgie. The two dogs have been together for years, so the vet is speculating that a brain tumor may be to blame. This story, and all those that have come before, illustrate how common shepherd ownership really is, despite the fact that I rarely see these dogs in my travels.

I received some fun pictures from my old friend, Eileen. She, like me, loves to talk about her dog. Her rescue dog,

Amiee, is her constant companion. In her e-mail, she recounted how Amiee came to her…"I'm sure you don't remember, but PD (her previous dog) arrived on the doorstep a week after I had been

attacked and bitten by a dog. I credit PD with rehabilitating me. After her work was done, she turned me over to Amiee, who has had much to teach me."

JANUARY 15

Errands today included a stop at the glass store to get picture frame glass cut. Since I was asked to wait, while the proprietor worked his magic, I asked, "Can I bring my dog in?" He said, "No. It's not safe with the glass." As I scoped out the showroom, there wasn't a single piece of glass that Cooper could reach, even if he wanted to. But I got it. He probably sees a lawsuit in the making. One place Cooper would be welcome is the pet store. Since we have CGC testing tomorrow, we need to mingle. That's never a problem at the pet store. Cooper is always offered a treat—which he may or may not accept. Today, a couple heaped an enormous amount of attention on Cooper. I thanked them for their kindness, as the husband and wife took turns greeting him.

We headed back to the car. As we entered the parking lot, Cooper watched intently as a woman and child approached. The child was in the midst of a major temper tantrum. As Cooper jumped in the back seat, the woman tried to soothe the child by having him "look at the big dog." That didn't comfort him in the least. We could hardly talk over the screaming. She did tell me that they have a German shepherd from Hawk Point Kennel. They board the dog at Valley Crest. I asked how her dog was with people and other dogs. She said he needs five minutes or so to warm up to people. Other dogs? Not so good.

John promised to go with me to a dog show in Piscataway, on the Rutgers Busch campus. Nancy had entered her Bernese mountain dog, Daisy, in the Novice Rally event. Unfortunately, we arrived too late to watch the team. Instead, we sat back as awards were handed out. There were Doberman pinschers, two enormous Irish wolf hounds, German shorthaired pointer.... You name the breed, it was represented. But one dog caught John's eye. As he pointed to the other side of the room, he said, "Look at that dog! Is that a Saint Bernard? It's beautiful!" I leaning right and left, to see what he was pointing at. When I finally locked in on the dog, it was Daisy. As the event came to a close, we waited to congratulate Nancy; she was holding an impressive rosette. She mentioned another AKC event in April at Round Valley Reservoir, just 10 minutes from home. I hated leaving Cooper behind today; indoor events don't allow un-entered dogs to attend. At Round Valley, we'll be outside. Cooper can then take in the sights with 100-plus dogs competing for Obedience and Rally titles.

As we drove home, I thanked John for making the trip. He was fine with it, since he really needed a break from what I fondly call The Labor Camp—our home.

January 16

Cooper is exactly 17 months old today, which means our intensive training has spanned 15 months. With that milestone, it was only fitting to test him for Canine Good Citizen certification. Knowing this day would come, it felt much like being back in college, before a final exam. I knew the subject matter, but the butterflies were still there. Cooper knows his subject matter—heel, sit, down, come, leave it.... To keep him in obedience mode, we got ready for Sunday training in the park. I donned insulated clothing for a very cold, 22-degree day, stuffing plenty of dried chicken strips in my pockets and set out for our big day. As we drove down to the park, I was momentarily confused, and then disappointed. No one was there. A lone car sat empty in the parking lot. Every Sunday for the past three months the parking lot had been filled with people, dogs, and puppies. We did a quick U-turn and headed home. Was this a good or bad omen?

Since I was already bundled up, I decided to take Cooper down to the river, a two-mile round trip. Not wanting him to rest too much before testing, we then played keep-away in the pen. Exercise continued inside, as I had him in a sit-stay in the living room, while I appeared to leave the house, to mimic the CGC separation test. I actually just rattled the door handle. On the first attempt, he broke his stay, racing toward me, as I stood at the door. Putting him back in place, we gave it another try. He was perfect. We were now ready to head over to the CGC test site.

When we got there, Cheryl handed me paperwork to fill out. I took Cooper and my clipboard to an open seat, as Cheryl whispered, "He can't growl at anything." That's one thing I hadn't considered. Would Cooper growl at a passing dog or person that gets too close? I was confident that this would not happen, but it remained in the back of my mind. When it was Cooper's turn, Renee came over to greet him. We shook hands and she commented on how laid back he was. As she crouched down to say hello, Cooper remained in place. She then said, "It's your turn." Since Renee loves German shepherds, she handled Cooper with ease. Cooper sat quietly as she began the test. In fact, within seconds, three tests were over. Again, Renee shook my hand, so Cooper accepted a friendly stranger. She moved in closely to pet Cooper, and then gently brushed him with the brush I handed her. Check. Check. Check.

Next, we went for a walk, following Renee. Cooper trotted along, no problem. Another check. The next exercise was walking through a crowd, which was a combination of volunteers and test-takers with their dogs. What was unexpected was the woman on crutches. This was really for therapy dog testing, but Cooper just kept his distance—no signs of aggression. We then waited for a Labrador to complete the recall exercise, so Cooper could take his place. The dog was on a 20-foot lead while the handler stepped back, and then called the dog; he would not budge. He sat there, as the young lady said, "Bailey, come!" over and over. It was comical. After they finally got him to move, it was Cooper's turn. I was hoping he wasn't watching that performance. He must not have been. Cooper was spot on. His stay, down and come were perfect; another check. The distraction test came next. How would he react to noisy pans dropped behind him? We walked to the other side of the room while Renee dropped the pans. This test was repeated again in the other direction. Cooper's reaction was somewhat startled, but he quickly regained his composure, which is what they want to see. He just couldn't turn and bark, or run for the door. None of that happened.

Cooper also had to walk by my side as Renee and her dog walked past. We shook hands and kept on walking; piece of cake. Check. The toughest test was yet to come—supervised separation. I left Cooper with a volunteer, held my hand up and said, "Stay! I'll be right back." Those were a tense three minutes. In that time, I bumped into a woman John and I knew years ago. Her beautiful standard poodle was at her side. As I pet her dog, I could hear Cooper whining. Was I threatening this last leg of the testing? Should I have just stood quietly? Perhaps she was there as the ultimate distraction. No. That would be paranoid to even consider. Soon, Cheryl turned around and said, "He's done." When I came around the corner, Cooper was right there. Had he dragged Renee across the room? Tell me it wasn't so. My concern was quickly extinguished when Renee extended her hand and said, "Congratulations! You passed!" Cooper had passed all 10 tests! We had done it! As we retrieved our belongings, people standing nearby said, "Congratulations!" It was a sense of accomplishment, 15 months in the making.

To celebrate, I splurged on a chicken quesadilla—oh, how Amy would disapprove. Cooper dined on dried organic chicken strips. When we arrived home, John was standing at the back door. Looking for my reaction, he said, "How'd he do?" With a sad face, I said, "He didn't make it." John's visible disappointment was short-lived as I quickly said, "He passed!" He gave me a big hug and kiss, patted Cooper on the head, and said, "Good dog!" As we entered the kitchen, Amy greeted us. She knew the news was good and hugged Cooper. It seemed that all was right with the world, for that one moment.

LESSONS LEARNED

✔ It's safe to say that German shepherds typically bond with one person in the family. If I leave Cooper at home with John and Amy, Cooper will not seek their company. Instead, he lies next to whichever door I left through. That's a characteristic of the breed that can be disconcerting to some. On the flip side, this attachment makes shepherds the ideal service dog.

✔ A dog should never bolt out of a car door. I'm more vigilant with Cooper, using the "Wait" command, until I can secure his leash in my hand. When I say, "Okay," he can exit. I'll never forget how John lost his grip on Cooper's leash at the Turkey Trot last year, sending a panicked puppy racing down Main Street.

✔ An animal-deterrent spray might, much like mace, provide a modicum of comfort while out and about with a dog. Stories of dogs attacking other dogs *and* people are not uncommon. I purchased SprayShield Animal Deterrent Spray on line (*www.dog.com*). Note that the manufacturer warns that it may not stop all animals.

✔ Dogs that know one another may still fight. This unexpectedly occurred at the GSD training in the park. Where was my animal deterrent spray when I needed it? In lieu of that, the book *Good Dog, Bad Dog,* has suggestions on ways to break up a fight.

1. If the dog is on-leash, use a corrective jerk of the leash, while saying, "No" in a firm tone of voice. For this to work, the collar has to be high on the dog's neck to feel the full impact.

2. If the dogs are already engaged, throw a garment or blanket over the more aggressive dog's head.

3. You can also take a water hose and spray the dogs, which can help break up a fight. But it's best to avert an encounter by observing the dog's body language. Signs of impending trouble include the dogs staring intently at one another, tail straight up or down, hackles raised, urination, barking, growling or scraping their hind legs.

✔ A business that appears to be dog-friendly may have a change of heart. Staples and The Eye Center are two such examples. I can understand the doctor's office, where patients may be frightened or have allergies.

✔ Good manners at the veterinary office are a wonderful thing. To encourage that behavior, I bring along a supply of treats. While Cooper was happy to snap up chicken strips in the waiting room, treats were of no interest in the exam room. He was more interested in the nearest exit.

✔ The AKC Canine Good Citizen certification is a great way to test your dog's ability to handle a wide variety of situations. It can also be a first step in achieving therapy dog status. For me, it was validation that we're making progress with a dog that was once afraid of his own shadow.

CONCLUSION

In October 2009, John and I were invited to a barn-warming party, which was thrown, in part, to acknowledge the architect, builder and contractors who worked on the massive construction project. A swank affair indeed, it was the event of the season—at least for us. Only days before, we had brought Cooper home. I hated leaving him behind that evening. But we thoroughly enjoyed the gourmet food, live country music and fireworks. We also made the acquaintance of a well-dressed couple. I'm not sure how we got on the subject of dogs. I probably said, "We have to get home to our puppy." When I told them that Cooper was a German shepherd, their eyes lit up. They had raised many shepherds over the years. I now wish we had talked longer. As we prepared to leave, there was a message the gentleman was eager to impart. He leaned across the table and said, "You are going to *love* that dog, and that dog is going to *love* you!"

When John and I got home, I wrote those words down on a scrap of paper, which is still in my nightstand. In fact, hundreds of similar scraps would follow, as I chronicled our life with a German shepherd. Writing became a form of therapy, as I was wholly unprepared for shepherd ownership. I never imagined that only a few months after that party, I would be weighing my options, including finding Cooper another home. That's about the time that another stranger said, "Don't give up on that dog!" I wish I could thank both of these wise men.

Simple words had a profound effect; they helped me make the right choice—to dig in my heels and do what was right. Letting this amazing animal down, and devastating my family, was not an option. That meant that I had to establish boundaries. Cooper was not going to take over our home. Once the atmosphere changed, and I became a confident pack leader, Cooper was more than willing to relinquish control. The result: no more barging through open doors, racing down stairs or barking uncontrollably at family and friends. Tormenting the cat is another matter.

In dog years, Cooper is not yet a teenager. Once he reaches four years of age, he'll likely be a couch potato. One thing is for certain, Cooper and I will continue our journey, with more advanced obedience classes and daily outings. Who knows, perhaps Cooper will add Companion Dog Sporting Program (CDSP), Rally, and Therapy Dog titles to his CGC certification. This big dog has limitless potential. Realizing that potential, however, requires a long-term commitment. So though Cooper has passed a critical test, it really just marks the beginning.

Afterword

So much has happened in Cooper's world over the past year. To keep the big guy in circulation, we have attended countless Obedience, Rally and K9 Nose Work classes. Doggy daycare is also a once-a-week event. While kicking around the house, Cooper is content to sleep, play keep-away with his toys or harass the cat. Meeko tolerates Cooper's relentless attention, which includes nibbling on his tiny back legs; clearly a herding maneuver.

When Cooper is outside, he's chasing down anything that moves. That included our landscaper, Jon. He was tasked with constructing a chain-link run, an enclosure that Cooper can't breach. As we stood in the driveway, discussing the layout, Cooper was loose in the yard. When Jon realized he needed rope to mark off the pen's footprint, he suddenly sprinted up the driveway toward his truck. Before I could say a word, Cooper was in pursuit. You know what happened next. Jon got nailed, a lightning fast nip to the derrière. Within seconds, Cooper was back at my side. Having returned, I couldn't reprimand him.

Cooper was doing what shepherds do. I've slowly come to realize *and* accept that fact. Cooper was likely being playful, certainly not vicious. There was no growling or barking involved. Jon didn't even appear startled. Instead, he turned to me with a big grin on his face. I yelled, "Are you okay?" He said, "Yes." In retrospect, Cooper was practicing an inherited skill. Just the day before, we had visited a sheep farm for herding testing. Cooper, and his littermate Molly, passed with flying colors.

Another activity Cooper thoroughly enjoys, besides annoying the cat—and various visitors—is K9 Nose Work.

This sport has gained in popularity. A dog of any size, breed or temperament can participate. Given the dogs natural scent-tracking ability, they excel at Nose Work. Cooper advanced from finding his favorite treat (dried lamb lung) to higher level training (birch scent), in preparation for his first K9 Nose Work Odor Recognition Trial (ORT).

The day of the trial, there were 50-plus teams anxiously awaiting their turn. When we were called to the floor, Cooper and I were faced with two rows of white boxes; I failed to count them, but 16 wouldn't be far off. I pointed to each box and said, "Is that it?" Still, Cooper was not focused on the task at hand. Then, out of the blue, he pawed a box and sat down—which was his signal that he located the scent. I said, "Alert!" to the judges, which is required. One of the judges responded, "Yes!" I quickly rewarded Cooper with a treat and said, "Good boy!"

Despite a shaky performance, Cooper had passed his first ORT in K9 Nose Work. And if this sport sounds easy, as I had once thought, it's anything but. The difficulty factor only increases. Interior searches with boxes are replaced with outdoor tracking, including vehicle searches. This sport combines challenging elements with *fun*. You also get to share in the successes of fellow dog owners and encourage others to try again.

While some might think I'm obsessed with Cooper, my husband included, I would counter that by saying I'm more obsessed with my iPhone. Amy urged me to get with the times. Little did I know that meant whiling away the evening hours checking e-mail, texting family and friends, and checking Facebook. John doesn't mind. He now has full control over the TV remote.

Even if I was obsessed with Cooper, I take comfort in knowing that I'm not alone. Baby boomers like me are apparently waiting for the day we become grandparents. Who knew? In the meantime, we shower affection on our pets, hence the term "grandpuppies." And since Amy has left the nest, enjoying her first "real" job and financial independence (something she called "overrated"), I have more time to spend with *her* dog. She would scoff at the notion that Cooper is hers, but that was the original plan.

Things turned out differently, no doubt. It's all good though. The dog that my brother not-so-affectionately called "a four-legged lawsuit" is now a certified therapy dog. Like Amy, Cooper now has a real job—bringing comfort to terminally-ill patients in the palliative care unit of a nearby hospital.

Reflecting back on this experience, I wouldn't change a thing. No, that's not entirely true. My search for a puppy should have extended beyond a single breeder, and included rescues and shelters. Many people I've meet over the last two-plus years have saved wonderful dogs—shepherds, Labradors, border collies, greyhounds—pure and mixed breeds alike. Regardless of origin, every dog needs strong, consistent leadership. As the holder of kibble and kindness, you are the center of your dog's universe; he wants nothing more than to please. Add daily structure, including lots of exercise, and you form a bond with your canine companion that is truly unbreakable.

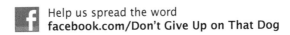 Help us spread the word
facebook.com/Don't Give Up on That Dog

Words of Wisdom

"Teaching our dogs to be well-mannered should not been seen as a desire to exert our will over them. It is vital to their safety and ensures that they will be warmly welcomed in their community and in our homes."

—Andrea Arden, *Dog Trainer*

"Training and building a relationship with your dog never stops."
—Martin Deeley, *International Association of Canine Professionals*

"One of the most prominent falsehoods is that once a puppy is house trained and has graduated from puppy-training class, a dog owner's work is done. Nothing could be further from the truth."

—Dr. Nicholas Dodman, *Dog Behaviorist*

"When working with dogs, you must always envision the positive outcome that you desire, which will allow you to turn any negative into a positive."

—Cesar Millan, *Dog Care & Rehabilitation Expert*

"In order to fully understand and effectively communicate with your dog, you must first learn to talk and think dog while seeing the world from the dog's point of view."

—Victoria Stilwell, *Dog Trainer*

"Saving one dog will not change the world, but surely, for that dog, the world will change forever."

—Author unknown

Acknowledgements

I wish to thank my editor, Diane Zediker-Pastore, former colleague and now Adjunct Professor at Seton Hall University. A stickler for detail, Diane has a formidable command of the English language and shares my love for animals. I have deep respect for her skills and greatly appreciated her help in refining this narrative.

No book is complete without a team of diligent proofreaders. Heidi Dabek, Marian Janes, Bonnie Ornitz and Diane Shallcross generously gave of their time, scouring these pages for the elusive typographical error. Never hesitating to give constructive feedback as well, I must express my sincerest thanks.

At my greatest time of need, Cheryl Smagala, professional dog trainer, provided much-needed guidance. From the moment I realized that we weren't in Kansas anymore, Cheryl provided the voice of reason. After many Obedience, Rally and K9 Nose Work classes, Cooper and I were thoroughly bonded and, thankfully, headed down the right road.

Kudos to Steve LaVallee who became my *Cesar Millan* from *Dog Whisperer* fame. Steve's visits to our home gave me the skills needed to be a calm, assertive pack leader. Without Steve's clear instructions on how to handle Cooper (at the first sign of trouble), our hopes of having a friendly, well-mannered dog could have been dashed.

A thank you also goes to a loose-knit group of German Shepherd Dog enthusiasts that meet in a nearby park. Year round, these dedicated shepherd owners brave wind, rain and snow to socialize their dogs, while reinforcing basic obedience exercises. Though Cooper was not from the same lineage as these dogs, the group leader and members always welcomed us.

For providing countless unscheduled "therapy" sessions, I thank Linda Wisniewski, doggy daycare owner, and her dedicated staff. They were never too busy to answer my questions, which gave me early insight into common behavioral issues, and how best to respond. And though he remains unknown by name, a wise doggy daycare client inspired the title of this book when he said, quite seriously, "Don't give up on that dog!"

Book & Article Resources

- Arden, Andrea, *Barron's Dog Training Bible*, Hunger Minds, Inc., 2012.

- Dale, Steve, *Good Dog! Practical Answers to Behavior Questions*, Tribune Media Services, 2011.

- Dodman, Nicholas H., Ph.D., *The Well-Adjusted Dog*, Houghton Mifflin Company, 2008.

- Dunbar, Ian, *The Essential German Shepherd Dog*, Wiley, John & Sons, Inc., 1998.

- Fogle, Bruce, D.V.M., *Dog Breed Handbooks: German Shepherd*, DK Publishing Inc., 1996.

- Goodspeed, Diane, *Happy Tails Across New Jersey, Things to See and Do with Your Dog in the Garden State*, Rutgers University Press, 2006.

- Grognet, Jeff, D.V.M., *Healthy Hips*, American Kennel Club Family Dog Magazine, Nutrition & Health (p20), Nov./Dec., 2011.

- McConnell, Patricia B., Ph.D., *The Other End of The Leash*, Random House, Inc., 2003.

- Millan, Cesar/Jo Peltier, Melissa, *Be the Pack Leader*, Three Rivers Press, 2008.

- The Monks of New Skete, *The Art of Raising a Puppy*, Little, Brown and Company, 1991.

- Siegal, Mordecai/Margolis, Matthew, *Good Dog, Bad Dog*, Henry Holt and Company, Inc. 1991.

- Stilwell, Victoria, *It's Me or the Dog: How to Have the Perfect Pet*, Hyperion Books, 2007.

WEB RESOURCES

- AKC Breed Rankings: *www.akc.org/news/index.cfm?article_id=4293*
- AKC Canine Good Citizen Program: *www.akc.org/events/cgc*
- American College of Veterinary Behaviorists: *www.dacvb.org*
- American Veterinary Medical Association Task Force on Canine Aggression and Human-Canine Interactions: *www.avma.org/public_health/dogbite/dogbite.pdf*
- Animal Behaviorist: *www.thepetdocs.com*
- Canine Noise Phobia™ Series: *www.throughadogsear.com*
- Clicker Training: *www.clickertrain.com/whatis.html*
- Crate Training: *www.humanesociety.org*
- Dog Daycare (NJ): *www.thepuppypatch.biz*
- Dog Laws: *www.dogbitelaw.com*
- Dog Nutrition and Health: *http://pets.webmd.com/dogs*
- Dog Products:
  - *www.cherrybrook.com* (Toll-free: 800-524-0820)
  - *www.dog.com* (Toll-free: 800-367-3647)
  - *www.drsfosterandsmith.com* (Toll-free: 800-381-7179)
  - *www.jbpet.com* (Toll-free: 800-526-0388)
  - *www.petco.com* (Toll-free: 877-738-6742)
  - *www.petvalu.com* (Toll-free: 800-738-8258)
  - *www.tractorsupply.com* (Toll-free: 877-718-6750)
- Dog Spaying & Neutering:
  - *www.spayusa.org* (Toll-free 800-248-7729)
- Dog Sports:
  - Agility (*www.usdaa.com*; 972-487-2200)
  - Flyball (*www.flyball.org*: Toll-free: 800-318-6312)
  - K9 Nose Work (*www.nacsw.net*)
  - Schutzhund (*www.germanshepherddog.com*; 314-638-9686)
  - Treibball (*www.americantreibballassociation.org*; 303-718-7705)

  Note: For additional information, Google *List of Dog Sports*.

- Dog Training:
  - Andrea Arden: *www.andreaarden.com* (212-414-5583)
  - Martin Deeley: *www.martindeeley.com* (407-469-5583)
  - Steve Hong: *www.k9key.com* (917-344-9838)
  - Steve LaVallee: *www.realk9solutions* (908-399-2551)
  - Cesar Millan: *www.cesarsway.com*
  - Br. Christopher Savage (Monks of New Skete): *www.newskete.com* (518-677-3810)
  - Cheryl Smagala: *www.trainingwithkindness.org* (908-479-4268)
  - Victoria Stilwell: *www.positively.com*

  Note: To search for a trainer/behaviorist in your area, visit
  - Association of Pet Dog Trainers: *www.apdt.com* (800-738-3647)
  - Animal Behavior Society: *www.animalbehaviorsociety.org* (812-856-5541)
  - International Association of Canine Professionals: *http://canineprofessionals.com/professionals/trainers*

- Donate & Volunteer:
  - *www.humanesociety.org*
  - *www.networkforgood.com*

- German Shepherd Dog Club of America: *www.gsdca.org*

- German Shepherd Rescue (NJ): *www.gsgsr.org*

- German Shepherd Rescue (CA): *www.gsroc.org*

- German Shepherd Rescue (TX): *www.agsdr.org*

  Note: To locate a GSD rescue in a state or area, Google, for example, *German Shepherd Rescue NY* or *German Shepherd Rescue New England.*

- Hip Dysplasia Statistics: *http://offa.org/stats_hip.html*

- Pet Adoption:
  - *www.humanesociety.org/issues/adopt*
  - *www.petfinder.com*
  - *www.petango.com*

- Pet Care: *www.peteducation.com*

- Pet Poisoning Helpline: *www.petpoisonhelpline.com/poisons/*

- Picking a Puppy: *http://www.martindeeley.com/*
- Puppy Lemon Law (NJ): *www.njcapsa.org*
- Raising a Confident Puppy, Kennels Von Lotta: *www.vonlotta.com/raising.html*
- Search Dog Foundation: *www.searchdogfoundation.org*
- Sheep Herding Instinct Testing (PA): *www.raspberryridgesheepfarm.com* (610-588-5262)
- Therapy Dog
    - Delta Society: *www.deltasociety.org* (425-679-5500)
    - Therapy Dog International: *www.tdi-dog.org* (973-252-9800)
- Top 10 Best Guard Dog Breeds: *www.petmedsonline.org/top-10-best-guard-dog-breeds.html*
- Top 10 Smartest Dog Breeds in the World: *www.petmedsonline.org/top-10-smartest-dogs-in-the-world.html*
- What is Schutzhund? *www.k9key.com/index.php/articles/64-what-is-schutzhund*

Note: The publisher is not responsible for websites—or their content—that are not owned by the publisher.

About the Author

S ince childhood, dogs have always been a part of Denine Phillips' life. From her first dog, Heidi, an energetic German shorthaired pointer, through seven much-loved golden retrievers, Ms. Phillips' New Jersey home is now shared with an odd canine couple–Cooper, an enormous German shepherd, and Ozzie, a mild-mannered Shih Tzu. Ruling the roost is Meeko, a 9-year-old Siamese cat that

Source: Star-Ledger Photographs © The Star-Ledger, Newark, NJ

showers affection on everyone and everything–except the dogs. Not long ago, Denine and her mother, Julia Waugh, enjoyed breeding and showing Maine coon cats.

Today, when not tending to her family and pets, Denine is a freelance technical writer with many published works to her credit. An expert in the field of document imaging solutions, she had the privilege to work in Tokyo, Japan, with one of the world's leading developers of office technology. That was in 2007, just as the economic downturn began to impact worldwide markets. With her penchant for writing, she turned to chronicling the many memorable moments raising a dog named Cooper.